Divorce 101

A Woman's Guide To Divorce

By
Tracy Achen

First published by AuthorHouse 04/08/04

ISBN: 1-4140-5148-4 (e-book)
ISBN: 1-4184-2565-6 (Paperback)

Library of Congress Control Number: 2003099703

This book is printed on acid free paper.

Printed in the United States of America
Bloomington, IN

Legal Disclaimer

No part of this manual may be reproduced or transmitted in any form by any means without prior written permission from the publisher or author.

The contents of this publication reflect only the author's views, and should not take the place of a lawyer, accountant, or financial planner. The explanations of legal concepts have been simplified to provide the basic principles of the divorce process, and should not be considered all-inclusive.

While every effort is made to ensure that the information contained in this manual is helpful and of high quality, no representation or warranties of any kind are made with regard to the completeness or accuracy of the contents of this manual.

As with any divorce, there are no guarantees of a certain outcome. The author is not engaged in rendering any legal professional service. The services of a professional divorce lawyer are recommended if legal advice or assistance is required for your particular situation.

Only a professional with specific knowledge about your situation and your state's divorce laws will be in a position to properly advise you. The publisher and author disclaim any personal loss or liability caused or alleged to be caused, directly or indirectly, by the use of any information presented herein.

Table of Contents

VI Splitting the Assets and Debts

VII Making Decisions About the Children

VIII Financial Support

IX Wrapping Things Up

I
Introduction

If your "Prince Charming" is really a frog, and "Happily Ever After" isn't, then it's likely that you are either considering a divorce or currently going through the divorce process. I would like to tell you that getting a divorce is a piece of cake, but unfortunately it's not.

Untying the knot is going to involve numerous decisions, and it's easy to feel overwhelmed by the whole process. Not only are there many choices to make when it comes to splitting your lives, but you also have to deal with the emotional turmoil that is common with the break up of a marriage.

They say that ignorance is bliss, but in a divorce, what you don't know can hurt you. It would be nice to think that your husband and lawyer will handle everything, but you are the one who is ultimately responsible for the outcome of your divorce.

The best thing that you can do is to arm yourself with the appropriate information in order to be prepared for what lies ahead. If you have the luxury of time, begin to plan for your divorce before it ever happens.

This book will help guide you through the no-mans land of divorce. It will provide you with the tools to stay on top of your situation so that you don't feel lost in the legal jungle.

You'll find answers to many of your questions about divorce. Get tips on choosing a lawyer, determining where you stand financially, and the various ways to approach dividing assets and debts. You'll also learn about custody arrangements, parenting plans, and visitation rights.

The information that you'll find outlines many of the situations that you will face in your divorce. Each state has its own individual divorce laws, and this is where the experience of a qualified divorce lawyer comes in handy. Use this book in conjunction with your lawyer to be prepared and knowledgeable about the divorce process.

To get the most benefit out of this guide, read it through once to get an idea of what you will be facing in your divorce. You can then go back through and fill out the worksheets to customize it to your own situation.

It is my hope that this guide will help make the divorce process easier for you. Please remember that the information contained within should not be construed as legal advice. For specific legal advice in your divorce case, you need to consult a skilled divorce attorney.

II
Preparing for Your Divorce

The Emotions of Divorce

Making the Decision

Are you thinking about ending your marriage? Are you bored with your life and disillusioned with your mate? Anger over a husband's actions, disappointment over failed dreams, and the drag of everyday life has pushed many people to throw in the towel on a marriage. The first thing that you need to realize is that getting a divorce won't solve all of life's problems.

In fact, you will probably be faced with a whole new set of problems because of the divorce, such as less financial stability and support. If you're looking for a change of pace, there are more constructive avenues. No one but you knows whether a divorce is the best solution for your situation. You need to really look into your heart and use logical reasoning to reach that decision.

You may be married to a man who is basically a good partner, provider, and father. If you still love your husband and just want your marriage to change, try marriage counseling before you talk about divorce.

Sometimes a stale and dying marriage can be brought back to life by pinpointing the problems and working on your marriage. Even if putting the extra effort into your marriage doesn't make it work, at least you can go into a divorce knowing that you gave it your best shot.

Bad timing for a decision

As a word of caution, don't threaten divorce unless you are actually ready to go through with it. Using emotional blackmail to get your husband to change can backfire on you if he decides to actually take you up on the threat. Divorce is no way to work out your problems, and the threat of it will bring no lasting changes in your husband.

It's also best not to make the decision to divorce in the heat of anger. We all know how emotions can swing, and reacting out of anger can leave your reasoning abilities clouded. You may be justified in your anger, but let that anger subside before you call your lawyer. Once you have cooled off and looked at the situation from all angles, then make your decision.

Ending your marriage because you love someone else

The same can be said about seeking a divorce because you are in love with someone else. You can't think clearly when you are in two relationships at the same time. If the feelings you have for this other person are genuine, put the relationship on hold while you deal with ending your marriage. True love will stand the test of time. Once you have ended your marriage and made peace with your feeling, you can see if you still want to be involved with this other person.

Don't look to be rescued from a bad relationship. Get out of it first so that you can heal your emotional wounds. Then you can think about dating again. Breaking off a love affair before you divorce is also a wise strategic move. If your husband knows nothing about the affair, he will be less inclined to use the divorce for revenge against you.

Your emotions

Going through a divorce may be one of the most stressful times of your life. Let's face it; just thinking about getting a divorce is the pits. There's the disappointment of knowing that your marriage just isn't working. Maybe you feel anger at your spouse for not living up to your expectations. There may be issues of abuse, infidelity, or substance addiction that have left your emotions raw.

If you are the one who decided to end the marriage, you may experience a lot of sadness. You probably took the vows of forever very seriously, and it's hard to admit that you can't live up to them. Sometimes you just can't make it work and it's better to move on.

It's common to feel guilty that you are putting your family through a lot of turmoil. It helps to remember that they would still experience turmoil if you were to stay in a bad marriage.

If your husband has served you with divorce papers out of the blue, it can be an incredible blow to your emotions. There's disbelief, hurt, anger, and the never-ending question of why. Even if the decision to divorce is mutual, there is a sadness that descends as you let go of the dream of a happy marriage.

The emotions you feel are very real and can swing from giddiness over the possibility of being free to the utter despair of feeling lost and alone. One of the best things that you can do for yourself is to get the emotional support that you need. Divorce is in essence the death of your marriage. Unfortunately, there is not the same community support for divorcing couples, as there would be for a death in the family. You will need to reach out to your circle of friends and family to get the emotional support that you need.

Talk to a trusted friend or family member about what is going on. Join a support group or talk to a counselor about what you are experiencing. Writing in a journal can also help you to release all the pent-up emotions that you are feeling. Eventually you will progress from merely surviving to healing, and from there you will begin your growth as an individual. Time allows you to heal.

Your husband's reactions

You may be totally floored by the way your husband reacts to your separation or divorce. He may come across as heartless and cold. He may do things that seem selfish, such as taking an extravagant vacation, buying a new vehicle, or ignoring the kids.

He may conveniently forget about promising to help support you while you are faced with the bill collectors and empty cupboards. Some can even turn violent, stalking and threatening you, especially if you are the one who initiated the divorce.

One of the most aggravating things that your husband may do is to make the changes that you so desperately wanted during your marriage. Why couldn't he have changed while you were still married?

Divorce jars some men to look in retrospect at their role in the marriage. Without having to fight the pressure from you to change, he can improve himself and his outlook without having his masculinity challenged.

Men and women react to divorce differently

While your husband's transformation during your separation and divorce can leave you standing there in utter disbelief, you need to realize that men and women react differently in matters of the heart. This doesn't mean that your husband is not feeling just as hurt and lost as you are, he just deals with the emotions differently.

A lot of men are naturally competitive, and winning in your divorce may be what is most important to him at this time. With this approach, your husband may set his emotions to the side for a while and approach your divorce like a business deal.

Even the man that turns into a sociopath is focused on coming out a winner. If you lived with a controlling husband, he can lash out and be mean when he realizes that you are not under his thumb any longer. Once the divorce becomes a reality, he can still seek control through threats, stalking, and legal maneuvers.

This is an extremely hard situation to deal with, but you have to stay strong and keep your emotional reaction to his antics to yourself. If you cave in or throw up your hands to his demands, he in fact wins.

Separating emotions from your divorce

Even if your husband doesn't act like a jerk, you need to go through the legal process of divorce with your emotions in check. Too many women end up with a less than satisfactory divorce settlement because they were so emotionally overwhelmed that they weren't able to concentrate on how their decisions would affect their future.

First of all, you need to accept that sometimes life isn't fair, especially when it comes to divorce. Next you need to decide that you will approach your divorce like a business deal. Keeping your emotions separate from your legal decisions may be hard, but it will ultimately serve you well in the long run. All the emotions will still be there, but you can deal with them separately by venting to your friends, support group, or counselor.

Approach your divorce with a level head

When it comes time to deal with the actual decisions to be made in your divorce, approach it as you would a business arrangement, concentrating on getting a fair and equitable settlement. Being in control and thinking with a level head will serve you much better than letting your heart lead your decisions.

Don't be surprised if your husband accuses you of being cold-hearted. Men are used to women caving in and going with the flow to keep everybody happy. The only problem is, if you give in during your divorce just to keep peace, you may end up with much less than you deserve. Gently explain to your husband that the divorce is not a personal attack against him, and that you are just trying to do what's fair. Separating your emotions from the critical decisions made during a divorce will help you focus on what is really important as you begin your new life.

Practical Preparations for Divorce

If you have been served with divorce papers, you need to see a lawyer immediately. If you don't respond to a divorce petition within the specified time frame provided for by the divorce laws of your state, then you lose the ability to contest the provisions outlined in the initial papers.

If you are just considering a divorce, but have yet to take any steps, a little planning can go a long way. Planning allows you to begin preparing for your life as a single person and avoid some of the post divorce pitfalls. You will also be able to gather the necessary information needed for your divorce case under friendly circumstances. Below are some pre divorce strategies that can help during the divorce and after everything is finalized.

1. You can consult a lawyer about your options without starting the actual divorce process.

2. Open a checking account in your own name. This will allow you to pay attorneys' fees and other expenses without you having to worry about your husband finding out or taking the money.

3. Begin to build a nest egg to cover emergency expenses, attorney fees, rent, deposits, utilities, etc.

4. Don't build additional debt, as you will want to keep assets as liquid as possible.

5. Don't quit your job, as you will need the financial security after you divorce.

6. If you don't already have a credit card, apply for one in your name only. It's much easier to establish credit before your divorce is finalized.

7. Make sure that all federal, state, and local taxes are paid to date. This can be a major hassle once the divorce is finalized. A tax lien is the last thing that you need as you start your new life.

8. If you suspect that your spouse has not reported taxes properly and stands to be audited, consider filing amended tax returns as married-filing separately.

9. Get a safety deposit box to store valuable documents and jewelry. Such items have a way of disappearing after a divorce is initiated.

10. Consider stashing sentimental items with a friend in the event that your spouse would destroy them out of rage.

11. It's a good idea to videotape your possessions, including the contents of your house, your vehicles, and other possessions. If things end up missing during the divorce, this can provide proof of its existence. It can also help jog your memory when it comes time to divide the marital estate.

12. Have important mail sent to a PO box or a friend's house.

13. If you are covered on your spouse's insurance, get complete medical and dental checkups done for you and the children. Have any necessary procedures done now while you are covered.

14. If you are covered on your spouse's insurance, start checking into getting your own coverage for health, automobile, and home.

15. Have your vehicle thoroughly inspected and repaired. Having costly repairs or needing to buy a new vehicle can crush your budget once the divorce is over.

16. Even though it may be tempting to just move out of the family home, check with your lawyer first to find out what the legal implications would be. In some states, it may hurt your chances of keeping the home after the divorce. It can also have an effect on the final custody decision.

17. If you are already separated, don't start dating. This will anger your spouse and decrease your chances of getting cooperation during the divorce.

18. Don't sign any documents before first consulting with a lawyer.

Financial Precautions

Divorce generally wrecks havoc on a woman's finances, but there are some steps you can take now to help protect yourself. First of all, don't sign any financial papers before first reviewing it with your lawyer or financial advisor. Stall for time so that you can make a copy and have it reviewed. Some husbands will start liquidating assets if they suspect a divorce is on the horizon. Money and assets have a way of disappearing.

You need to begin building your independent financial status before your divorce. At this point you need to start considering how you will handle your finances, protect yourself from liability, and retain a good credit rating.

<u>Seek financial and legal advice</u>

It's a good idea to consult with a CPA or financial planner before you ever begin divorce proceedings, especially if you and your husband have been married quite a while or have a lot of holdings. They can help advise you on strategies for dividing the marital, in addition to tax planning and any financial moves you need to make before the divorce is finalized.

In some states there is an automatic restraining order prohibiting either party from transferring, withdrawing, borrowing against, or changing the beneficiaries of any marital assets once the divorce papers are served. With this in mind, it is wise to separate your financial lives before papers are served. If you have your paycheck deposited into a joint account, transfer it to a new account in your name only.

You are generally entitled to half of the value of all joint accounts in most states. Your lawyer may advise you to take half of the money, and then close the joint accounts.

This protects you in the event that your spouse decides to clean out the account in reaction to divorce proceedings. It also protects you against overdraft charges should your spouse write hot checks.

<u>You can be held financially responsible for your husband's actions</u>

If your name is on the account when a check bounces, you will be held responsible. If you are going to withdraw half of the funds, be sure to make a copy of the account statement showing the full balance. Then make a copy of your withdrawal slip showing your half of the money. Also copy the deposit slip showing that your half of the money has been deposited in a separate account.

Check your credit

Now is also the time to get your credit in shape. You should get a credit card that is in your name only. Also, get a current copy of your credit report from each of the three credit bureaus (TransUnion, Exeprian, and Equifax). This allows you to check for any outstanding loans, inaccurate information, and delinquent accounts.

It comes as a shock to many women that they will be held responsible for joint debts after the divorce is finalized. Therefore, it is important to know where you stand. For delinquent accounts and judgments, contact the individual companies to settle the accounts and update your credit file. For inaccurate information, request an investigation to have your files updated.

Protecting your credit

If you and your husband are separated or a divorce is imminent you might consider putting a freeze on home equity credit lines and other credit accounts. Send creditors a letter by certified mail requesting that a freeze be put on joint accounts.

State that you refuse to be responsible for charges made after the date of the letter. Remember that you won't be able to close the account until the balance is paid off.

To also protect yourself against further liability, you might also consider publishing a disclaimer of liability for your spouse's future debts in your local paper. Publication in the newspaper is generally sufficient notice to third parties in most states of your refusal to accept liability for your spouse's future debts.

Dirty Divorce Tricks

Unfortunately, divorce can bring out the worst in some people. In some cases, a spouse is more concerned with winning than being fair and will try all sorts of ploys to come out on top. This is not to say that your husband will do this. You just need to be aware of some of the dirty tactics that have been used in past, ranging from emotional blackmail to unethical financial moves. This list illustrates some of the unethical moves that have been made in divorce cases.

While it is never advocated that you use any of the following maneuvers, it's a good idea to watch out for the tricks that may be played against you.

- Threatening to seek custody of the children. This is the emotional trump card in most marriages. If your husband has generally been uninvolved in the children's lives, this ploy is a way of getting you to agree to certain provisions just so that you won't have to fight for custody.

- Selling off joint assets to friends or family before divorce papers are filed. In this case the assets will usually be returned to your husband after the divorce is finalized.

- Draining joint bank accounts before filing for the divorce.

- Running up huge credit debts on joint accounts before the divorce, knowing that both of you are liable. Worse yet, using cards in the other spouse's name to do this.

- Opening a bank account in another state in order to hide funds.

- Claiming that the house that you both labored over to fix up (and therefore increased its value) is separate property since he owned it before your marriage. The increase in value can be claimed as a joint asset.

- Offering you an equal value in junk bonds and speculative stocks while he retains the blue-chip stocks. In the long run, your husband's stocks will have a higher value (and be worth more money)

- Asking his employer for a pay-cut or to be paid some money under the table so that child-support payments will be less.

- Using your guilt (if you initiated the divorce) to get you to settle for less. Just because you want the divorce, doesn't mean that you should get less than your fair share.

- Insinuating that all the fighting over property and children is destroying the possibility of future relations. You may hear "After all we've been through together, do we have to tear each other apart like this? Let's try to work things out and just be friends." The only problem is that most people tend to give in too easily for the sake of the friendship.

- Threatening suicide to make you feel guilty so that you won't push certain issues.

- Refusing to pay any bills or support while you are negotiating a settlement in an effort to force you into accepting his conditions.

- Filing a restraining order to keep you out of the family home.

Separating Before Divorce

Sometimes a couple will try a trial separation before they actually make a commitment to divorce. This gives them the chance to see what it is like to live apart and if they really want to make the split permanent.

Separation agreements

Even if it is just a trial separation, you should consider getting a separation agreement to protect yourself. This can help insure that the bills are paid and that there are no disagreements over how things are handled. It also helps protect you when things turn out nasty in an otherwise friendly split.

Unfortunately, not all states recognize a legal separation. Delaware, Florida, Georgia, Idaho, Mississippi, Pennsylvania, and Texas are states that do not recognize a legal separation.

A separation agreement outlines where you and the children will live, addresses temporary child support and alimony, how the assets will be split, bills paid, and mail handled. A legal separation also helps protect you against being held responsible for your spouse's debts, liabilities, and taxes after the date of separation.

Protecting your credit

During your separation, it is wise to maintain separate bank accounts. It is also wise to send copies of your separation agreement to your bank, broker, creditors, and any other financial institutions that you and your spouse do business with.

Consider putting a freeze on all joint credit accounts and send a letter stating that any changes to joint accounts will require both signatures.

Drafting your separation agreement

Just as with a divorce, you should have a lawyer to advise you and draw up your separation agreement. A separation agreement is legally binding and may also set precedence in your future divorce case.

Courts will generally assume that if you managed with the provisions of the separation agreement, then there should be no reason for any big changes in your divorce settlement (if it's contested). You should put just as much thought into your separation agreement as you would into a divorce agreement.

If you have drawn up a suitable legal separation agreement, you may have the option of converting it into a divorce agreement. There may be additional requirements to convert your legal separation into a divorce decree, depending on the state that you live in.

Domestic Abuse

If domestic abuse has occurred in your marriage, whether it's emotional or physical, it may have an effect on your divorce. Domestic abuse has nothing to do with love or hate. It's all about control. If you decide to divorce your husband, you will be taking away his control, which can lead to a volatile situation. This is why planning is so critical before you file for a divorce from an abusive partner.

<u>Planning</u>

You need to be prepared before you ever announce that you want a divorce. Have a plan to protect yourself and your children should your husband react violently as you start to break the ties. Below are some suggestions to help you prepare for the break:

- Copy all important documents such as bank account and credit card information, birth certificates, marriage certificates, social security numbers, pay-stubs, and medical and insurance information. Keep them in a safe place, such as a safety deposit box or with a trusted friend.

- Keep evidence of physical abuse, such as pictures, a detailed journal of the abuse, and restraining orders in a safe place.

- Set money aside to help you get by and find a new place to live. If possible, open your own checking account.

- Have a spare set of keys, clothing, and essentials stashed with a friend or at a safe place.

- Get a post office box to have important mail forwarded to.

- Contact your local shelter to arrange placement in a safe house.

- If you have already contacted a lawyer, be sure to explain your situation. Your lawyer can't help you unless he knows what is really going on.

Making the break

When it comes to leaving an abusive situation, you need to realize that it may spark rage in your husband. If you are threatened, you may need to get a restraining order, but be aware that this may push some men over the edge.

The most dangerous time for an abused woman is the first 24 hours after a restraining order has been issued. Some men feel that they won't be controlled by a piece of paper. If you do get a restraining order, ask the police if they can drive by your house, or contact your local shelter to see if you can stay at a safe house until things are settled.

Taking your children

If you are planning on leaving the family home, take your children with you. You may be afraid to do this because your husband has previously threatened that he will never let you take the children.

From a practical standpoint, consider how it would appear to a judge if you left your children in a potentially dangerous situation. Also consider the power that you would be handing over to an already controlling husband.

He could keep you from seeing your children and therefore have the best form of leverage in negotiating your divorce settlement. In essence, he might say that in order for you to see your children again, you'll need to agree to his terms.

Getting legal help

When you make plans for your divorce, you will want to hire a lawyer that has experience in divorces involving domestic abuse. You need someone that understands the dynamics of such a relationship and can help prevent you from being intimidated into an unfair divorce agreement.

If your case goes to trial, you need someone who can enlighten the judge about your circumstances, and will be willing to protect you and your children.

How domestic abuse affects divorce

Once your divorce begins, there are a few points to keep in mind. In states where fault is a consideration in the divorce process, the evidence of domestic abuse can influence the property settlement as well as custody and visitation arrangements.

While mediation is generally suggested as the first method of resolving divorce disputes, it's not appropriate in cases where there has been domestic abuse. If your state has a mandatory mediation clause, you can ask the court to wave mediation due to the domestic abuse.

Custody arrangements

You also need to seriously consider whether joint custody would be the best arrangement in your case. This is because with joint custody arrangements open the door to continuing contact with your ex-husband, which may not be a safe situation.

Abusers often use custody and visitation issues to try to establish or continue control over their spouses. If custody is being disputed, make sure that the courts know about the abuse, because it will have a bearing on the best interests of the children and the structuring of custody and visitation. Courts are uncomfortable with denying visitation with the non-custodial parent, but may order supervised visitation in cases of domestic abuse.

Divorce is a crazy time anyway, but when you add the pressures of a volatile situation to it, it can seem unbearable. To help cope, try to find a support group or get some counseling to help you during this time. Your local shelter can provide a lot of support and resources for you. Don't be ashamed to ask for help.

Dating Before Divorce

If you're thinking about dating before your divorce...DON'T! You may think that you are free to start a new relationship once the decision is made to separate or divorce. But it is wise to hold off on the dating scene until after your divorce is finalized for a number of strategically, legal, and emotional reasons.

<u>Strategical reasons not to date before divorce</u>

Emotions are raw during a divorce. When you start seeing someone else, it is like rubbing salt into your husband's wounds. Believe me, he will likely react to the fact that you are dating by making your life hell during the divorce process. He may seek revenge to compensate for the anger, hurt, and embarrassment that he feels you have caused him.

Even if your husband has carried on numerous affairs during your marriage, he will not think that you are justified in seeing someone new at this time. All he will focus on is that he has been wronged and will want to seek justice anyway he can. He may try to even the score by fighting about custody of the children or how to split the marital estate.

If you have children, then you also need to realize that it's in your best interest to try to keep a cordial relationship with your husband. You will most likely have ongoing contact with your husband after the divorce because of the children.

Dating during your divorce can poison the spirit of cooperation and affect your life for a long time after the divorce is final (and possibly after your boyfriend is history).

<u>Legal reasons not to date before divorce</u>

As far as the courts are concerned, you are still legally married until the divorce is finalized. In states that recognize fault in a divorce case, dating during your divorce can be viewed as adultery. This can affect the outcome of your divorce as far as child custody and visitation, spousal support, and the eventual property settlement.

Even if you have been separated from your husband for a while, dating during your divorce can be used to help prove marital misconduct during your marriage. It can look like you have questionable morals, even if you were the perfect wife during your marriage.

Your new mate may be open to scrutiny

To top it off, a really vindictive husband might consider suing your boyfriend for alienation of affection. This will put your boyfriend smack-dab in the middle of your divorce, which is a quick way to put a damper on your new relationship.

You need to be especially careful if you have children from your marriage. Not only will both you and your husband's conduct be scrutinized during a custody case, but also so will be the conduct of your boyfriend. If he has a shady background, it will be used against you.

Any person who has frequent contact with your children can become part of a custody investigation. If there are past issues of domestic violence or charges of sexual misconduct (proven or not), it will have repercussions in your divorce.

Your level of support may be lowered

Another consideration that you should think about if you are considering living with your boyfriend is that it will affect the level of support you may eventually receive. Even if you ultimately get custody of your children, child support levels may be lowered because you are living with someone and sharing the expenses.

It can also have a big impact on whether or not you will receive alimony and how much you receive. This can even apply to temporary support order, because once again, you are sharing the expenses with someone else. It would be a shame to forfeit your future support on a relationship that may not last.

The bottom line is that if you date during your divorce, you are giving your husband a big advantage. Don't sacrifice your future on a new relationship. Wait until after the divorce is finalized before you start to date.

Emotional Reasons Not to Date During Divorce

When you are separated or going through a divorce, the attention a new man shows you can feel like a breath of fresh air and boost your self-esteem. Your boyfriend may serve as a distraction to help you avoid the feelings of pain that normally result from divorce. You will eventually need to face those emotions, though.

While it feels good to be needed and wanted, it's unlikely that you're emotionally ready to deal with a new relationship. You will still have to deal with all the issues of your marriage and make peace with the pain from its breakup.

A new relationship at this time is not really going to be based on the real you. Imagine how differently you will act when you are not under extreme stress and when your life is more stable. You need time to discover that you can make it on your own without a man to support you emotionally or financially.

A boyfriend can be great to boost you up and help you deal with things, but once the dust has settled, where does that leave him? You won't need him in the same ways that you did before the divorce. All the support and attention that were welcome before may become stifling afterward. On the other hand, some men just aren't willing to put up with all the problems that go along with a divorce and will cut free as soon as they get the chance.

If you have children, it is especially important to focus your emotions on them right now. Divorce is scary for kids. If you are dating, it will confuse them and threaten what little stability that they perceive. They can feel pushed aside and unloved because you are spending time with your boyfriend. Give them the attention that they need right now. Your love life can wait. Besides, you'll be in a better position to enjoy it later.

What if he really is the one for you?

I know that your emotions are running high right now, but you need to consider reality. When you are going through a divorce, you're usually not in a mental state to make permanent choices. Studies have shown that the first relationship that a person enters into after a divorce has little chance of long-term survival and will rarely end in marriage.

So what should you do if you believe that this new man is the one you really should have married in the first place? Make life easier on you and him both by postponing the relationship until the divorce is finalized.

If he truly is as special as you think, then he will be willing to wait. Once all the papers are signed, you can resume the relationship and see if it still feels the same. If it doesn't, you have saved both of you a lot of heartache.

What if you are determined to continue the relationship anyway? I would seriously recommend talking with your lawyer. Your relationship might not have much bearing if you have had a long separation from your husband, don't live in a fault state, and your divorce is uncontested. Even then, follow your lawyer's suggestions and keep the relationship under wraps and out of the public eye. Even though it may seem like your divorce is taking forever, you owe it to yourself to not stir up the dust.

III
Getting Your Information Together

Gathering the Required Documentation

From the time you start a divorce until it is finalized, you will be asked many questions that will require detailed and accurate answers. The worksheets throughout this manual can serve as a reference to all these questions. It will take some work to gather all the information and documents, but it will help your lawyer with your case and give you a good understanding of your situation.

It is wise to begin collecting as much information and documentation as soon as you consider a divorce or feel that your husband will be seeking a divorce. Collecting this information will save you time in the long run, keep you organized, and help you to understand everything involved in your divorce. You will stand a better chance of getting all the information if your marriage is still on friendly terms.

<u>Documents to have on hand</u>

It is a good idea to make copies of the following documents and keep them in a safe place:

- Current income tax returns with W-2s, 1099's, and all other reported income (interest, dividends, etc.).

- Your husband's most recent pay stub, as well as the name, address, and phone number of his employer.

- Your husband's drivers license number and social security number.

- Titles and registration to all vehicles.

- Deeds and mortgage papers to all properties

- Wills, life insurance policies, pensions, and retirement fund papers and statements.

- Health and dental insurance policies and cards

- Bank and credit card statements, CD's, and savings account information.

- Loan statements

- Business records

You can begin the process of gathering information by working on personal information about you and your spouse first. This is the information that your lawyer will need to begin your case and will help process your paperwork more quickly.

Personal Information and Records

Your lawyer requires a lot of information when you initiate a divorce. You can save yourself time by filling out the following worksheets before you ever meet with your lawyer. You can also determine the income for both you and your husband, to make it easier to calculate child support and alimony later on in your divorce. Determining your living expenses will help you grasp your financial situation and establish a budget that allows you to live within your means after your divorce.

Information	Self	Spouse
Full Name		
Maiden Name		
Date & place of Birth		
Social Security #		
Education dates and degrees		
Passport number		
Current Address, City, State, Zip Code		
Length of residency in this state		
Home Phone		
Work Phone		
Cellular Phone		
Driver's License # and state		
Employer		
Work Address, City, State, Zip Code		

Information	Self	Spouse
Criminal History, Arrests, and Convictions		
Wages or Salary		
Work Benefits Health Insurance **Life Insurance** **Profit Sharing** **Retirement** **Bonuses**	1. 2. 3. 4. 5.	1. 2. 3. 4. 5.
Active Military?	Yes___ No____	Yes___ No___
Retired Military?	Yes___ No___	Yes___ No___
Branch of Military		
Year entered military service		
Domicile address when first enlisted		
Current base assignment		
Current Rank		
Any Previous Marriages?	Yes___ No___	Yes___ No___
Date of prior marriage (s) and spouses name		
Date of Prior Divorce (s)/ Death of Spouse		

Current Marriage Information: (include a copy of marriage license and any prenuptial or ante nuptial agreements, as well as separation agreements)

1. Date of Marriage _____
2. Place of Marriage _____
3. Age at Marriage: Self_____ Spouse_____
4. Prenuptial Agreement? Yes _____ No_____
5. Length of separation _____
6. Previous filings for divorce _____
7. Restraining orders _____

Information about the Children: (note - have a copy of their birth certificates on hand)

Name	Date and place of Birth	Sex	School and grade level	Social Security Number	Is Child From a non-Marital or Previous Marriage?
1.					
2.					
3.					
4.					
5.					

Insurance policies:

Type	In Who's Name?	Company	Policy #	Address	Phone
Life Insurance	**Owners Name** _____ **Beneficiary** _____				
Auto ins.					
Auto ins.					
Auto ins.					
Home ins.					
Health					
Health					
Disability					
Umbrella Policy					

Income Worksheet

Note: Having the last three years state and federal income tax statements can help you fill out this section.

Income	Self	Spouse	Joint
Gross monthly Income-salary and wages			
Bonuses and Fringe Benefits			
Social Security Benefits			
Retirement Income			
Disability Payments			
Unemployment			
Workmen's compensation			
Welfare			
Child Support From a Previous Marriage			
Dividends			
Income from trusts & annuities			
Royalties & Residual Income			
Interest Income			
Business Income			
Rental Income			
Other income			
Totals:	$_____	$_____	$_____

Income Deductions	Self	Spouse	Joint
Federal Taxes			
State Taxes			
Social Security			
Unemployment Insurance			
Medicare Deduction			
Insurance Deduction			
Retirement or Pension Fund Deduction			
Savings Plan			
Union Dues			
Child Support Deductions			
Other			

Total Deductions: $_____ $_____ $_____

Calculating Net Monthly	Self	Spouse	Joint Income
Gross Income	$_____	$_____	$_____
Total Deductions	$_____	$_____	$_____
(Subtract total deductions from gross Income)			
Equals Net Monthly Income	$_____	$_____	$_____

Calculating Your Living Expenses

Along with all the other personal information and documentation, you should also calculate your monthly living expenses. In cases involving child support and/or alimony, you will need this information to determine the levels of support that will be awarded. It can also be useful for setting up a budget once the divorce has been finalized.

Can you live on one paycheck?

You need to assume that the living expenses will have to be met by your income alone after the divorce. If your expenses total more than your income, this is where support, debt assumption, and settlement payments can help even things out. You may also have to find ways to cut back on your expenses after your divorce. While it may be discouraging, this exercise can be a real eye-opener.

To help figure out what your expenses are, take the time to go through at least one year's worth of cancelled checks and receipts. This can help to remind you of expenses that only occur once or twice a year, such as taxes and fees. You may also need to go over your tax statements to find information that may not be noted in your checkbook. Also look at your bank statements for check charges and any other fees that come directly out of your account. Fill in the information on the following page, and add any expenses not listed at the bottom.

Rent /Mortgage	$_____	Allowances	$_____
Home Ins	$_____	Kids Lunches	$_____
Property Taxes	$_____	School Tuition	$_____
Gas	$_____	School Supplies	$_____
Electric	$_____	Tutoring	$_____
Phone	$_____	Team Fees	$_____
Cable	$_____	School Photos	$_____
Water	$_____	Daycare	$_____
Trash	$_____	Camps	$_____
Sewer	$_____	Recreation	$_____
Internet	$_____	Sports Fees	$_____
Cell Phone	$_____	Club Dues	$_____
Storage Fees	$_____	Gifts/Cards	$_____
Groceries	$_____	Cleaning Goods	$_____
Eating Out	$_____	Office Supply	$_____
Pocket Cash	$_____	Bank Fees	$_____
Doctor Bills	$_____	Checks	$_____
Dental	$_____	Safety Deposit	$_____
Eye Care	$_____	Credit Cards	$_____
Prescriptions	$_____	Bank Loans	$_____
Clothing	$_____	Auto Loans	$_____
Barber	$_____	Tax/Title/Lic	$_____
Nails	$_____	Auto Gasoline	$_____
Magazines	$_____	Auto Ins	$_____
Newspaper	$_____	Tires & Maint.	$_____
Pet Care	$_____	Tolls	$_____
Child Support	$_____	Health Ins	$_____
Repairs	$_____	Life Ins	$_____
Services	$_____	Entertainment	$_____
Charities	$_____	Other	$_____

Total Monthly Expenses $_____

IV
Getting Legal Help

Do You Need a Divorce Lawyer?

In the United States, there is no universal divorce law. Each state has its own specific laws regarding marital status, property division, child support, and alimony. For this reason, if you have children or a large number of assets or debts, it is wise to retain a lawyer familiar with the laws of your state. A skilled divorce lawyer can help guide you through the divorce process.

Can my husband and I use the same divorce lawyer?

If your husband has already presented you with divorce papers, you definitely need to retain a lawyer, if nothing else other than to review the paperwork for you. You need your own separate counsel (not the same lawyer your husband is using) to protect yourself.

Even if you and your husband are able to agree to the terms of your agreement, using the same attorney can be a big mistake. First of all, a conflict of interest occurs for the attorney. There is no way to represent both sides of a case fairly. If you are the one who has hired the lawyer, he will consider you his client and word the settlement agreement to protect your interests. Likewise, a lawyer hired by your husband will protect your husband's position.

A good divorce lawyer will strongly urge that legal council represent both sides. This helps assure that the divorce decision won't be appealed or set aside at a later date. There is nothing worse than to have your finalized divorce reopened because both sides weren't adequately represented. Think twice before you consider using the same lawyer for your divorce.

Can I obtain a divorce without a lawyer?

If you and your husband decide that you don't want to involve lawyers, there are instances when you can represent yourself in your own divorce.

This is called a "pro se" or do-it-yourself divorce. Pro se divorces can be time consuming and not all courts and judges are receptive to these cases.

If you are considering representing yourself, first establish how receptive your local court system is by visiting with the country clerk and asking how the court views self-representation. If there seem to be no obstacles in filing your own divorce, you can find divorce kits at many office supply stores or on the Internet.

The minimal requirements for a do-it-yourself divorce are that:

- **Both parties mutually agree that it is best to divorce.**
- **You have been married a relatively short period of time.**
- **There are no minor children involved.**
- **There are very little assets or debts, and you both agree on how everything should be split.**
- **Your spouse has not yet retained a lawyer.**
- **Neither spouse is active military.**
- **Each spouse is capable of supporting him or herself.**
- **There is no impending bankruptcy.**
- **There is no history of abuse or intimidation.**
- **You have the time to fill out the paperwork and do the necessary court filing.**

If the above circumstances apply to your situation, and you feel comfortable handling the legal paperwork, you can proceed with a pro se divorce. If you run into snags or want to check your papers for accuracy and completeness, you can hire an attorney to review and file your paperwork for you.

If representing yourself is too much of a hassle, or if your situation is complicated, then it is best to have legal representation during your divorce.

Choosing a Divorce Lawyer

The lawyer you choose to represent you will act as your legal advisor. By applying the relevant divorce laws of your state, your lawyer can help you decide what you want from your divorce and how you should negotiate your settlement. It is important therefore to choose a lawyer with whom you are comfortable and who knows divorce law. So where do you find a good divorce lawyer?

Find a lawyer who specializes in family law

You first want to focus on finding a lawyer who specializes in family law. Look at it this way, if you needed open-heart surgery, would you choose a doctor that specializes in general medicine or a heart specialist? The same goes for your divorce. Look for someone who has experience with family law. This is an important step in your life and it should be handled by the most qualified legal representation that you can afford.

If you already have a lawyer who handles other legal matters for you, ask for a referral. Your lawyer will likely know someone who specializes in family law that has a good reputation. You can also ask your divorced friends for references, contact the local bar association, or look in the phone book for lawyers that handle divorces.

Setting up an interview

Try to set up an initial interview with at least three attorneys. The initial interview is usually free or relatively inexpensive, but it will give you a good overview of what you will be facing. The time spent searching for and interviewing potential lawyers to handle your divorce will always be time well spent. Your lawyer will be handling one of the biggest decisions in your life.

It is important to note that as you go through the initial interview and discuss your case with a lawyer, he or she will not then be able to subsequently represent your spouse. This is an important consideration when you are starting a divorce. If your spouse doesn't yet have a lawyer, it would be to your advantage to interview who you deem to be the best lawyers first.

When interviewing prospective lawyers, it helps to look at it as if it was a job interview and you are the employer (which in essence you are). As you go through the interview, ask yourself whether you can afford their rates and whether you are comfortable with how they suggest handling your case.

A good lawyer will start out by negotiating first and save the threat of a trial as a last resort. Ask prospective lawyers how they will proceed with your case, what would be a fair settlement, and how much it will cost. Ultimately, who you retain as your lawyer will depend on who you feel will handle your case in the manner you wish at a price that you can afford.

What should you do if your husband has filed divorce papers in another town or even another state? You might consider interviewing lawyers that practice in that district. This is because local lawyers are familiar with the area's court systems and judges, and are familiar with the other lawyers that practice family law.

Getting the best lawyer for your case

Once you have narrowed down your search, your interviews will give you insight on who will best represent you. Remember that a lawyer can only advise you on what actions to take in your divorce, while you are the one who will make the final decisions. Therefore, you want a lawyer that you feel comfortable working with so that it is a team effort. Take your time and interview more than one lawyer.

Your lawyer is the person who will be representing you and guiding your legal battle. Be open and honest with your lawyer, and don't be afraid to ask questions. This is the only way to find out what you are entitled to.

Your lawyer can help guide you and suggest strategies, but you are the one who ultimately calls the shots. Hire someone who you are confident will be part of your team. You want a lawyer who really hears what your concerns and questions are. The following worksheets will help you make that choice as you begin interviewing lawyers.

Lawyer Interview Worksheet

Name   Office Hours   _____

Law Firm   Appointment date _____

Address   Appointment time _____

Phone Number

What percentage of your practice is family law?
_____

How long have you practiced divorce law?
_____

Do you know or have you ever represented my husband?
_____

Who will be handling my case?
_____

How long will my case take?
_____

How much will this cost?
_____

What is your hourly rate?
_____

How is court time charged?
_____

What is your billing schedule?
_____

How much is the retainer/ is it refundable?
_____

Do you have a retainer agreement?
_____

Do you encourage phone calls?
_____

Will I be billed for phone calls & how much?
_____

What are the best times to reach you?

_____

How quickly can I expect phone calls to be returned?

_____

When is the best time to schedule meetings?

_____

How will my case be handled if you are out of town? Whom can I contact?

_____

What if I can't meet during normal business hours?

_____

Will you keep me informed on the status of my case?

_____

What is expected of me?

_____

What can I do to help in my case?

_____

Can I file for temporary maintenance, child custody, and child support?

_____

Are you experienced in custody litigation?

_____

What strategies do you suggest for getting a fair settlement?

_____

Will I be able to get alimony?

_____

What is your preferred method of settling disputes?

_____

Do I have a choice of courts, and does it make a difference?

_____

General impressions:

Do you feel comfortable talking to the lawyer?

_____

Does the lawyer seem optimistic about your case?

_____

Is the lawyer straightforward about your situation?

_____

Notes: _____

Retaining and Working With Your Lawyer

Retaining a lawyer

The time spent searching for and interviewing potential lawyers to handle your divorce will be time well spent. Once you have chosen your lawyer, you should discuss what the various expenses and retainer fee will be. You will also need to sign a retainer agreement. This in essence is a business agreement between you and your lawyer. It outlines what services will be performed, the fee schedule, the retainer fee, and whether it is refundable or not. There will also probably be disclaimers of any guarantee of the outcome of your divorce. You also want to establish whether you will receive copies of all your paperwork and a summary of everything you have been billed for once your divorce is finalized.

Retainer fee

A retainer is a fee that you pay up front to start the divorce process. It acts as a deposit from which your lawyer will withdraw the various fees and billable hours. Anything over and above this will be billed separately. Generally you will get a monthly statement outlining what has been done on your case and the corresponding charges. When your retainer has been used up, you will then need to pay for the extra fees and hourly bill.

The cost of divorce

You may be wondering what your divorce will cost you. The costs of getting a divorce vary widely from area to area, depending on how long your divorce takes, whether it goes to trial, and how much your lawyer charges. Ask your lawyer for an estimate of how much your divorce will cost. Even though you may request that your husband pay for your legal fees as part of your divorce settlement, you will generally have to pay the retainer fee up front to get the case started.

Working with your lawyer

Your first meeting with your lawyer helps set the groundwork for your divorce. There should be a clear understanding of what you want from your divorce and what your lawyer expects of you. Given what you are expecting, your lawyer should outline what he feels will be the best strategy for your case. If you are being unreasonable in your expectations, your lawyer should tell you.

The quickest way to have a long, drawn-out divorce is to ask for all the marital assets, plus custody and support, and then not be willing to budge in the negotiations. Your lawyer will probably suggest ways to reach a fair and equitable agreement.

You may not agree with everything that your lawyer suggests. If it is something that you feel strongly about, ask your lawyer the reasons for his suggestion. It may be that what you are asking for would not be granted if your case went to court. Your lawyer may also offer strategies and compromises to get what you want. The main thing is to talk with your lawyer and be realistic about what you want.

Don't use your lawyer as a therapist

It can be tempting to vent all of your frustrations to your lawyer to, but you would be better served by doing this with a friend or counselor. First of all, your lawyer is charging you by the hour and your retainer fee will be eaten up really fast. Secondly, venting doesn't help the progress of your case. It may feel good to let someone know just how badly you have it, but unless it directly relates to the case, it's a waste of valuable time.

As your divorce progresses, don't be surprised if you get disappointed and frustrated. Divorces have a way of dragging on, especially when you are waiting for a response from your husband's lawyer or to get on the court docket for a hearing. Don't take it out on your lawyer.

If you feel like you are being left in the dark, call your lawyer's office and ask for a progress report. Also realize that sometimes your lawyer will have bad news for you. Maybe your husband won't budge on an important issue or is requesting something that's totally outrageous. Instead of going into a rage, sit down with your lawyer and discuss what your options are. Remember that your relationship with your lawyer is all about teamwork and communication.

Changing Lawyers

There are times when a lawyer and client just can't work together. You can seriously hurt your final divorce settlement by keeping a lawyer that you are unable to work with. Before you think about replacing your lawyer, make sure that you have communicated your dissatisfaction both in person and in writing. Remember that your lawyer can only give you advice; he can't guarantee the outcome of your case. Give your lawyer a chance to discuss possible solutions to what you perceive as the problem. Ultimately, you make the final decisions in your divorce.

Getting a second opinion

It might be in your best interest to get a second opinion or consider changing lawyers if you are not being adequately represented. This might be the case if your lawyer refuses to follow your wishes (as long as they are within the law) or is not attending to your case in a timely manner. Maybe there is a conflict of interest due to prior dealings your husband had with your lawyer.

Unprofessional conduct

Unfortunately, some lawyers cross the line with their clients by suggesting illegal activities or by making sexual advances. Also, if your lawyer doesn't conduct discovery in your case, doesn't notify you of hearings or trial dates, or worse doesn't show up himself, it is definitely time to seek new counsel. You want to be represented by a lawyer who is both ethical and on the ball.

If your lawyer is jeopardizing your case, it is definitely time to seek new counsel. For recourse, you can file a complaint with the state bar association if your lawyer has damaged your case, not filed the proper papers, failed to file paperwork in a timely fashion, forged your signature, etc.

When to switch lawyers

Of course, the earlier in your case that you choose to switch lawyers, the better. Generally, it's not a good idea to change lawyers in the middle of your divorce case. If you think about it, it will cost you another retainer fee and it will take extra time for the new lawyer to be brought up to speed on everything that has transpired in your case.

How to change lawyers

To change lawyers, you will need to send your current lawyer a letter stating that you no longer need his or her services. State that you will come by the office to pick up your case file, and that you will need a refund of the remaining retainer (if it was written in your retainer agreement that the retainer was refundable). Your case files can then be given to your new lawyer to continue the divorce proceedings.

Your lawyer also has the option of quitting before the case is closed. To do this, your lawyer would need to file a notice of motion to be relieved as your counsel. If you don't oppose the motion, you will need to retain another lawyer and file a pleading with the court for a substitution of attorney. This lets the court and your husband's lawyer know that another attorney will represent you.

Collaborative Divorce

Collaborative divorce is a fairly new method of reaching a divorce settlement. The aim of Collaborative divorce is to avoid litigation and minimize the financial and emotional impact that normally accompanies divorce. Collaborative divorce tends to be more non-combative than traditional approaches to divorce, thereby reducing post-divorce hostilities. It is a means of reaching a peaceful resolution to the issues of a divorce.

How does Collaborative divorce work?

In a Collaborative divorce, both the husband and wife are represented by their own lawyer. What is unique is that both lawyers agree to withdraw from the case if it becomes adversarial. This helps everyone strive to reach agreement on the divorce issues. There is an open exchange of facts and documents, so there is no need for formal discovery. The goal is to reach a fair settlement through open negotiations without the threat of a court trial.

When is Collaborative divorce appropriate?

A Collaborative divorce might be a good option in cases where the decision to get a divorce is mutual and both sides agree to cooperate. In such cases, both the husband and wife, along with their respective lawyers and the assigned judge will sign an agreement to a Collaborative divorce.

When is Collaborative divorce not appropriate?

Collaborative divorce is probably not the best option for marriages where one spouse has been abusive or very controlling. There needs to be a fair and open exchange of ideas and opinions during a Collaborative divorce without the fear of intimidation.

It is also not a good idea to seek a Collaborative divorce if one spouse is prone to hiding information. Collaborative divorce requires full and truthful disclosure of information on a voluntary basis.

<u>What are the advantages of Collaborative Divorce?</u>

This method of divorce is less time consuming and costly than an adversarial divorce. Everything is resolved through negotiations, eliminating the need for formal discovery and removing the threat of going to trial. The couple, eliminating the need to hire two sets of advisors, hires all divorce advisors, such as accountants, therapists, and financial advisors jointly. Collaborative divorce does not pit one side against the other and spouses are more likely to walk away from the divorce satisfied with the outcome.

<u>How is Collaborative divorce different from mediation?</u>

In mediation, both spouses meet with a neutral mediator to negotiate their divorce issues. After a preliminary resolution is established, each side then discusses the proposed agreement with their lawyer. The mediator can't assist either side, and issues are discussed only if someone brings it up. In Collaborative divorce, both spouses and their lawyers sit down together to work out the details of the divorce. If you feel overwhelmed by the situation, you know that your lawyer is there to speak up for you and your interests.

Collaborative divorce is an option for the couple that wants to end their marriage as peacefully as possible. Spouses use their lawyers for guidance rather than as their gladiators in a divorce battle. When a settlement is reached jointly, both sides are more likely to be satisfied with the outcome of their divorce.

V
Understanding the Legal Aspects of Divorce

The Divorce Process

Once you have retained a divorce lawyer, you then begin the legal process of divorce. The divorce process can be extremely frustrating because legal issues have a way of seeming to drag on forever. Once you've made the decision to divorce, it's understandable that you want to get it over as soon as possible. The best advice is to just be patient, and if necessary, express your concerns with your lawyer about how long it seems to be taking.

The legal process of divorce establishes that your marriage is indeed over, how the assets and debts will be divided, the determination of child custody, child support and visitation, and if any alimony or family support will be awarded. The basic divorce process is as follows:

I.   **Divorce Petition or Complaint** - This document notifies the court and your spouse that you want the court to end your marriage. It outlines the grounds for divorce, and the proposed property settlement. The person who initiates the divorce process is called the petitioner (or plaintiff) and the other spouse is called the respondent (or defendant). Where the divorce petition is filed depends on the residency requirements of each individual state.

II.   **Response or Counterclaim** - Your spouse is entitled to file opposing papers. In some states, if your spouse doesn't file a response within a certain time period, he will lose the right to negotiate the terms of the divorce and have no right to object later.

III. **Temporary Rules** (pendente lite orders)- This sets the ground rules while the case is pending, such as:
      • Who will stay in the house?
      • Who is responsible for the children?
      • Who is responsible for certain bills?
      • Restraint against inappropriate conduct.
      • Assignment of temporary relief and child support.

IV.   **Discovery** - This is the legal procedure for obtaining information and documents from your spouse, which can be accomplished through voluntary exchanges of information, interrogatories, and dispositions.

V. **Conflict Resolution** - If you and your spouse cannot reach an amicable settlement, you have various options to settle disputes. These include private meetings, mediation, arbitration, or going to trial.

VI. **Settlement Agreement** - The final agreement between both parties covering division of assets and debts, child custody and support, visitation, alimony, and any other items you want included in your divorce.

VII. **Final Judgment or Decree** - The final document, which will be signed by the judge that officially ends your marriage.

Individual state laws affect how long your divorce will take and how it will proceed. Individual state laws also determine how assets, debts, and support payments are assigned, so it is very important to know some of the basic divorce laws in your state. You will find many state tables as you work through the following sections.

Separation and Residency Requirements

Some states require a period of separation before a divorce will be granted. There are also requirements that you and your spouse live in that state for a certain period of time before you can file for divorce in that state. If either spouse meets the residency requirements of that state, even if one spouse lives elsewhere, then the courts of all states will recognize your divorce. The following table will help you locate your individual state so that you can determine the residency and separation requirements.

State	Residency Requirements prior to filing	Separation Requirements	Recognizes legal separation
Alabama	6 months or 180 days		Yes
Alaska	30 days		No
Arizona	90 days		Yes
Arkansas	60 days	18 months	Yes
California	6 months		Yes
Colorado	90 days		Yes
Connecticut	0 to file/ 1 year to be finalized		Yes
Delaware	6 months		No
District of Columbia	6 months	1 year unless both agree	Yes
Florida	6 months		No
Georgia	6 months		No
Hawaii	3 months to file/ 6 months to be finalized		Yes
Idaho	6 weeks		No
Illinois	90 days	2 years unless both agree	

State	Residency Requirements prior to filing	Separation Requirements	Recognizes legal separation
Indiana	6 months		Yes
Iowa	12 months		Yes
Kansas	60 days		Yes
Kentucky	6 months		Yes
Louisiana	12 months		Yes
Maine	6 months		Yes
Maryland	12 months unless grounds occurred in MD	1 to 2 years	Yes
Massachusetts	12 months unless grounds occurred in MA		Yes
Michigan	6 months or 180 days		Yes
Minnesota	6 months or 180 days		Yes
Mississippi	6 months		No
Missouri	90 days	24 months	Yes
Montana	90 days	180 days unless both agree	Yes
Nebraska	0 if lived in NE the entire marriage/ 1 year otherwise		Yes
Nevada	6 weeks		Yes
New Hampshire	12 months		Yes
New Jersey	12 months	18 months	Yes
New Mexico	6 months		Yes
New York	12 months	1 year	Yes
North Carolina	None to file/ 6 months before final	1 year	Yes
North Dakota	6 months	1 year if spouse denies no-fault	Yes
Ohio	6 months		Yes
Oklahoma	6 months		Yes
Oregon	6 months		Yes
Pennsylvania	6 months	2 years unless both agree	No
Rhode Island	12 months		Yes
South Carolina	3 months if both are residents/ 1 year otherwise	1 year	Yes

State	Residency Requirements prior to filing	Separation Requirements	Recognizes legal separation
South Dakota	None, but one must live in SD until divorce is finalized		Yes
Tennessee	6 months	2 years unless both agree	Yes
Texas	6 months		No
Utah	90 days		Yes
Vermont	6 months	6 months	Yes
Virginia	6 months	1 year with children/ 6 months no children	Yes
Washington	None		Yes
West Virginia	None if married in WV/ 12 months otherwise	1 year unless both agree	Yes
Wisconsin	6 months		Yes
Wyoming	None if married and live in WY/ 60 days otherwise		Yes

Grounds for Divorce

The person who files the initial divorce papers must state the grounds for divorce. The terms "fault" and "no-fault" refers to the reasons behind the divorce.

No-fault divorce

If you want a divorce, you can get one without fault having to be proven. A <u>no-fault</u> divorce is one in which neither spouse blames the other for the break up of the marriage. There is no defense to a no-fault divorce and you cannot be prevented from getting such a divorce. All states now offer some form of no-fault divorce. Common basis for a no-fault divorce includes:

- Irreconcilable differences
- An irretrievable breakdown of the marriage
- Incompatibility
- Separation with no intent to reconcile

Fault divorce

Two-thirds of the states still offer some form of fault divorce. The spouse asking for the divorce must prove that an act by the other spouse proves marital misconduct and provides a legal reason for the divorce. Fault divorces are usually sought in cases where one spouse will benefit because of the fault, such as with obtaining child custody, increased support, or a better settlement. If you are seeking a fault divorce, good record keeping will help your case. Keep evidence such as police files, restraining orders and violations, any convictions, dates and photos of abuse, and evidence of affairs in a safe place.

The following are common grounds for a fault-divorce:

- Abandonment or desertion
- Cruelty - physical or mental suffering that makes living with the abusive spouse unbearable
- Insanity
- Conviction of a crime
- Alcohol or drug addiction
- Impotence

- Adultery - valid in 28 states
- Gross neglect of duty

The following table has individual state information and how it may relate to your state as far as fault issues are concerned.

State	No Fault	Fault	Not Compat- ible	Living separate and apart	No alimony for spouse at fault	Fault affects the split of assets
Alabama	x	x	x	2 years		x
Alaska	x	x	x	2 years		
Arizona	x					
Arkansas		x		18 mos		
California	x					
Colorado	x					
Connecticut	x	x		18 mos		x
Delaware	x	x	x	6 mos		
District of Columbia				1 year		
Florida	x					
Georgia	x	x			x	
Hawaii	x			2 years		
Idaho	x	x				
Illinois	x	x		2 years		
Indiana	x		x			
Iowa	x					
Kansas	x		x			
Kentucky	x			60 days		
Louisiana	x			6 mos	None if spouse commits adultery	
Maine	x	x				
Maryland	x			2 years		x
Massachusetts	x	x				
Michigan	x					
Minnesota	x					
Mississippi	x	x				

State	No Fault	Fault	Not Compat-ible	Living separate and apart	No alimony for spouse at fault	Fault affects the split of assets
Missouri	x			1-2 yrs		
Montana	x		x	180 day		
Nebraska	x					
Nevada	x		x	1 year		
New Hampshire	x	x		2 years		x
New Jersey		x		18 mos		
New Mexico	x	x	x			
New York	x			1 year		
North Carolina	x			1 year	x	
North Dakota	x	x				
Ohio	x	x	x	1 year		
Oklahoma	x	x	x			
Oregon	x					
Pennsylvania	x	x		2 years		
Rhode Island	x	x		3 years		
South Carolina		x		1 year	x	x
South Dakota	x	x				
Tennessee	x	x		2 years		
Texas	x	x		3 years		
Utah	x	x		3 years		
Vermont		x		6 months		
Virginia		x		1 year		
Washington	x					
West Virginia	x	x		1 year	None if spouse commits adultery	
Wisconsin	x					
Wyoming	x		x			

As you can see, determination of fault can have an economic bearing in some states. Discuss legal strategy with your divorce lawyer to see whether you need to file your divorce as a fault divorce or a no-fault divorce.

Contested, Uncontested, and Default Divorce

Uncontested divorce

An uncontested divorce is one in which both spouses agree to the divorce and are able to work out the issues of the divorce without going to court. The divorce settlement may be reached through mutual agreement or by going through some form of mediation or negotiation. Once a settlement is agreed upon, the state specific divorce forms are filed with the court and the judge can finalize the divorce.

Default divorce

A default divorce may be granted when one spouse is served with divorce papers, but fails to respond to the divorce complaint. This may be due to his or her agreement with the terms of the divorce. Another instance in which a default divorce may occur is when there is the inability to locate a missing spouse. If you can't locate your spouse, many states will require proof that a diligent effort has been made. This may include notifying relatives and employers. At the least, you will need publication in a newspaper to serve as notification of your intent to divorce.

Contested divorce

A contested divorce occurs when both spouses cannot reach agreement on the terms of the divorce. Contesting a settlement proposal involves negotiation, mediation, arbitration, or going to court to resolve the disputed issues. This can be expensive, especially for court litigation. You may need to hire investigators, subpoena witnesses, and have appraisals done. Expect to pay your lawyer more for the extra hours put into your case.

Overall it is less expensive and emotionally taxing to avoid going to trial, but there are situations that may merit a judge's decision in your case. Just be aware that this approach takes the power of choice out of your hands and allows decisions concerning your life to be put in the hands of a third party.

Temporary Rules/ Interim Orders

Temporary rules, also called interim orders, outline how things will be handled until the divorce is finalized. Generally, your lawyer will suggest the filing of some sort of temporary orders. Some of the issues that temporary rules address are:

- Temporary custody of the children
- Temporary child support
- Visitation schedules
- Temporary family support
- Restraining Orders

Temporary family support

If you rely on your husband's income to pay the bills and buy food, it would be wise to file for temporary support (pendente lite relief). This motion asks the court to require your husband to continue supporting you until the divorce is finalized. If your husband is served temporary orders for support, but doesn't keep up with the payments, you can include a provision in your divorce settlement to make up for the arrears.

Temporary custody

It is also a good idea to request temporary child custody and child support, especially if you want the children to live with you after the divorce. If the court eventually decides custody issues, judges are reluctant to disrupt the status quo, especially if you're the one who has always cared for the children.

Temporary child support

In regard to any temporary child support that you request, try to have it set at a reasonable level that truly reflects what it costs to raise a child. You can get a rough estimate by consulting your state's child support guidelines. If the amount is set low in your temporary child support orders, your husband may argue that you have managed to survive on this amount without requesting an adjustment.

With this argument, the judge may see no reason to raise the levels. Keep this reasoning in mind in the determination of pendente lite relief as well.

Restraining orders

You may also seek to get a restraining order at this time. If your husband is abusive or violent, it can help to have a court order barring abuse and harassment.

Restraining orders cover more than protection against abuse. They can also restrain a spouse from freezing bank accounts, tying up assets, or transferring property. You can also request that utilities cannot be disconnected or insurance dropped without an application to the court.

It's important to remember that even if you get a restraining order preventing your spouse from entering the home, you should still have the locks changed. Divorce can make people do crazy things, and you need to protect yourself and your belongings. Contempt of court charges may be brought if your spouse violates the restraining order.

Either spouse can file for temporary orders

Temporary orders are available to whichever spouse seek them. Once temporary orders are in place, they have the full effect of the law. If they are broken, contempt of court charges may be brought, and the violating spouse may face jail time.

Bifurcated Divorce

Sometimes spouses want to end the marriage immediately, but still have issues that are not yet satisfied in the settlement agreement. In these instances, the couple may choose to seek a bifurcated divorce.

What is a bifurcated divorce?

A bifurcated or divisible divorce is one in which the marital status is terminated by the court while settlement agreement issues such as child custody, support, alimony, and property division are decided at a later date. Usually one hears about a bifurcated divorce in connection with high profile marriages, but ordinary people can obtain a bifurcated divorce as well. Because some divorce cases can take months to resolve, couples may seek to have their divorce divided in order to have their marital status changed as soon as possible.

This may be the case when one spouse is seeking to remarry, or wishes to be declared single for tax purposes. Sometimes one spouse drags out the settlement agreement as a form of emotional blackmail, knowing the other spouse cannot get on with his or her life until the marriage is finalized. Another situation in which a bifurcated divorce may be sought is when an automatic stay is put on the divorce proceedings due to a bankruptcy action.

Not all states allow a bifurcated divorce

Because state laws vary on the subject of bifurcation, a person considering this route should consult with their lawyer to see if it is allowed in their state and what restrictions there are. Some states, such as Michigan, Nebraska, Arizona, and Texas do not allow a bifurcated divorce.

A court order is required for a bifurcated divorce

To have your divorce bifurcated; you must get a court order to do so. The decision to bifurcate your divorce case will be at the discretion of a judge, who will schedule a hearing to decide whether bifurcation is appropriate in your case. Realize that obtaining a bifurcated divorce will be more expensive, due to increased lawyer fees, litigation and court costs.

Military Divorce

If you or your husband are in the military, it would be wise to retain a lawyer who has experience in military divorces. Military divorces sometimes take longer due to the fact that a military spouse is entitled to sufficient time to respond to the divorce petition. Most courts will usually grant a stay of proceedings if the military spouse is in basic training, advanced training, or overseas. A military divorce also has extra considerations, such as:

1. Domicile or residency requirements for filing. This is because the jurisdiction of your divorce is based on domicile. With an enlisted person, domicile may be determined by the legal residence of the military spouse, the legal residence of the other spouse, or the state that the military spouse is stationed in.

2. Obtaining service on an active duty spouse. It is necessary to personally serve an active duty spouse with a summons and divorce petition. This may be hard if that spouse if stationed overseas. To accomplish this, you will need to give your lawyer your husband's social security number and a copy of his orders.

3. Compliance with military rules and regulations. These include the Soldier's and Sailor's Civil Relief Act, the Uniformed Services Former Spouse's Act, the 20/20/20 Rule, the 20/20/15 Rule, and the Military Cobra Plan

4. Division of military pensions. If the military pension is divided as property (as opposed to alimony) the nonmilitary spouse can receive the monthly payment directly from the Defense Finance division.

5. Continuance of spouses' benefits. Depending on the number of years married during active duty (at least 10 years), the nonmilitary spouse may qualify for certain base privileges and medical and dental benefits, until that spouse remarries.

As you can see, a military divorce needs to be handled by an experienced lawyer who understands the rules and regulations governing military divorces. Your divorce will also be affected by whether the jurisdiction is in a community property state or an equitable distribution state.

Discovery

What is discovery?

Discovery is the process in which information is exchanged between each spouse and their respective lawyers. During divorce proceedings, you have the right to see (and have copies of) all of your spouse's financial records. Each spouse is generally required to fill out a statement of net worth that contains all the relevant facts about your finances and property. Discovery can help reveal unknown assets and get everything out in the open.

Informal discovery

It is generally to everyone's advantage to disclose the requested information voluntarily. The informal discovery process begins with the information that each spouse provides his or her lawyer. Your lawyer may then request information from your spouse's lawyer to get a complete picture of the financial situation. Each spouse may be required to provide tax returns, loan applications, bank and credit card statements, business records, title transfers, property information, and anything else deemed relevant.

Using experts in the discovery process

If needed, your lawyer may also suggest hiring an actuary to determine the value of pension plans. Appraisers can also be brought in to determine the value of a business or other important assets.

If there are hidden assets

Unfortunately, some spouses don't willing provide all the financial paperwork in hopes of coming out ahead in the settlement agreement. One way in which assets can be hidden is by opening savings accounts in the children's names or a joint account in a relative's name. Money and titles can also be hidden in safety deposit boxes that you may be unaware of. Discovery can be a means of getting the whole financial picture out in the open.

Means of formal discovery

Formal discovery methods may be used if either lawyer feels that there is some information that is not being disclosed voluntarily. Lawyers may use interrogatories, depositions, and subpoenas to collect the necessary information. The advantage of formal discovery is that it provides a factual record on which to base your settlement agreement. If, at a later date, it is determined that assets were not disclosed, the settlement agreement may be modified (if fraud is established).

A deposition is a means in which a lawyer can formally question a spouse. The conversation is recorded and can be used in court at a later date. Lawyers may also use interrogatories to obtain information from the spouse. Interrogatories are written questions that require a written response from the other side. These are often used to clarify areas of concern. This is a formal procedure and all questions should be answered truthfully so as not to commit perjury. Another way to get information is with a subpoena. Financial records, documents, and witnesses can all be subpoenaed to get the full picture.

Overall, it is better for all parties involved to voluntarily provide the information requested. It saves both time and money, not to mention stress.

What Is Decided in a Divorce Settlement?

Some people are overwhelmed by all the decisions that need to be made during a divorce. Unfortunately, life doesn't prepare you to make these important decisions while your world is turned upside down. The best thing that you can do at this time is to not let your emotions guide your decisions. It has been said that you should approach your divorce as if you were making a business decision.

Factors affecting your divorce settlement

It may be relatively simple to reach a settlement agreement if you have not been married very long. Your divorce settlement will be affected by whether you live in a community property state or an equitable distribution state. It is also relevant if there are minor children, and the amount of marital assets and debts. As your life gets more complex, so will your divorce.

If you have children, decisions will need to be made regarding child custody and support, parenting plans, and visitation schedules. You'll also need to determine who carries insurance on the children and who gets to claim them as dependents for tax purposes. Unfortunately, this is one area of a divorce that is hard to agree on and it may ultimately have to be decided by a judge if an agreement can't be reached.

Splitting your assets and debts

You'll also need to decide how the assets and debts are divided. Again, the more you have, the more complex the decisions will be. You'll need to decide how to split retirement accounts, property, business interests, and debts. Other decisions will need to be made concerning alimony, transferring property, name changes, and any provisions for future changes to the agreement. All of these items can be decided in the settlement negotiations.

You can request that your spouse pay your lawyer's fees

You can also request that your husband pay your attorney's fees as part of your settlement agreement. This is a common practice when one spouse doesn't work or earns substantially less than the other spouse.

Settlement proposals

It helps if the negotiation process begins right from the start. You need to discuss what you want from your divorce with your lawyer as soon as possible so that he can draw up a settlement proposal. Your husband's lawyer will likely also draw up his own settlement proposal. After settlement proposals are exchanged, it is common to have a meeting with all involved parties to begin negotiations. In the next section, there is a discussion of various negotiating strategies.

Negotiating Strategies

Settlement negotiations are the part of your divorce where you and your spouse work out the nuts and bolts of how assets and debts will be divided, what the custody and child support arrangements will be, and any other specifics that will be included in your divorce decree. Negotiations can occur in the lawyer's office, over the phone, through mediation, or by mail correspondence.

Before negotiation begins

There are two parts to divorce negotiation: what is affordable and what is acceptable. The objective is to find a balance between the two. It is unrealistic to expect that you will be entitled to everything from the marital estate.

Begin planning your negotiating strategies with your lawyer by determining what you want and what your lawyer feels is reasonable to ask for. Your lawyer will probably suggest some negotiation strategies to help you get what you want.

Be professional when negotiating

When negotiating, try to separate personal matters from the business at hand. You need to approach negotiations from a position of strength to be effective. It doesn't help to get emotional when you're trying to be firm about your requests. You need to approach your settlement negotiations in a professional manner in order to obtain the best possible outcome.

Be forewarned that your husband may accuse you of being cold-hearted and ruthless. Try to visualize how your husband would handle a business deal. Most likely he would take a direct and practical approach without caving in to just save the other person's feeling. You need to do the same. Just remember that you are negotiating a settlement that will affect your future (one without your husband in it). Look out for yourself.

Negotiation is About Compromise

It helps to think of negotiation in terms of compromise. Consider what you actually need and what you are willing to give up. Negotiations often begin with written offers and counteroffers. This can help avoid heated confrontations between you and your husband and also will also prevent you from giving in due to feelings of guilt.

Written counteroffers will allow you time to discuss your options with your lawyer and help prevent you from making hasty decisions just to get it over with.

If negotiations are done between parties in a lawyer's office, be aware that everything doesn't need to be settled in one day. Don't be forced into a decision that you're not comfortable with. Reschedule another appointment if you need to. This will allow you time to discuss your objections or concerns about the proposal with your lawyer in private.

Start on common ground

Plan to start your negotiations by focusing on what you know that you both agree on. As you reach agreement on certain issues, consider these issues off-limits to further negotiation. If you don't, negotiations can start going in circles with nothing ever being settled. You will eventually come to issues on which you don't agree. This is where you can use some of the other negotiating tactics.

Asking for more than you expect

During negotiations most people start out by asking for more than they expect to receive. This tactic leaves room to bargain, with the aim of the eventual outcome being close to each side's bottom line. Also, by asking for more that you expect to receive, you might just get it, especially if your spouse doesn't feel that it is worth fighting over.

Consider bartering to even things out

Don't give something away until you are sure that you can trade it for something else that you want. If there is disagreement over something specific in the marital estate, consider bartering for something else of equal value.

For instance, if both you and your spouse want to keep the family home, you might offer that you keep the home and your spouse keeps the family business. If neither one of you is willing to concede on a certain assets, an option is to sell it and split the proceeds.

Another way to approach dividing the marital estate is to take the net worth (as determined in the worksheets from the assets and debts section) and split the total to determine how much value each spouse is entitled to. Then you and your spouse take turns picking assets and debts until a relative balance is reached between each side.

Reality check

If things begin to get bitter, you might need to concede on certain issues. If you and your husband are fighting over every little thing (such as who gets the cat and who gets the sheets), you need to step back. At this point, your negotiations are probably more about revenge than closure.

Ask yourself what is really important to you, then focus on that and let the rest go. If you can easily replace the items that your husband is asking for, let him have them.

When negotiations stall

The aim of settlement negotiations is to reach an agreement that you both can live with. Even though you may not be able to reach total agreement, you have established a basis for the things that you do agree on. When you feel that no further progress can be made through informal negotiations, you may want to consider other forms of conflict resolution, such as mediation, arbitrations, or going to court.

Try to reach a settlement out of court

You need to realize that all of these methods involve extra expense and time. As a rule of thumb, try mediation before arbitration or having your settlement decided by a judge. This is because the emphasis is still on reaching an agreement between the parties as opposed to a decision being made by a third party that doesn't know the needs of the individuals.

Ultimately, settling out of court is almost always better. It is less expensive and time consuming. It also saves the children further emotional turmoil and reduces the animosity that you will later feel towards your husband.

As you can see, there are many ways to negotiate your divorce settlement. If there comes a point in which negotiations stall, you might then consider using mediation to resolve the issues.

Mediation

Mediation is an effective alternative to court litigation for resolving those issues that you and your spouse just can't work out. A mediator represents neither side, but acts as a facilitator to help you and your spouse work through the issues and reach a mutually agreeable settlement.

<u>Benefits of mediation</u>

A big advantage to mediation is that is voluntary and allows both of you to retain control over the outcome of your settlement agreement. One benefit of mediation is that the proceedings do not become part of your divorce record. Settlement is reached quicker and creative solutions are achieved, as compared to a court trial, which can be pretty cut and dried. It is also much cheaper than going to court.

Many courts now require mediation on issues relating to the children. In mediation, the focus is on the best interest of the child, not the individual wants of the parents. To locate a mediator, you can ask for a referral from your lawyer, or ask friends and associates who have been through mediation who they would suggest using. You can also call your local bar association for a referral.

<u>Finding a mediator</u>

You want a mediator who has a lot of experience with divorce cases and who doesn't have a relationship with either you or your spouse (remember that you want the mediator to be impartial). Many mediators are lawyers or mental health professionals who can help couples begin to truly communicate for the first time.

During your initial interview, you can find out what the mediator's hourly fee is, how it will be billed, what time frame will be involved, what the mediator's training and experience is, etc. A good mediator is one who is a good listener and communicator who can present creative solutions to your problems.

<u>Beginning mediation</u>

Mediation usually starts off with a session to get acquainted with the couple and the issues that need to be resolved. The mediator will also explain how mediation works and whether it will be appropriate in your case. The next step may be to talk with each individual to get a perspective on the case.

Once the issues and positions are determined, the mediator can discuss available alternatives that the couple may not have considered. The mediator also helps both spouses discuss the issues in an open manner, helping them work toward a mutual agreement without taking sides. A good mediator discourages intimidation tactics and pushes toward cooperation.

Reaching a settlement through mediation

It's a good idea to discuss any settlement proposals that arise from mediation with your lawyer. He or she can advise you about the consequences of the proposals. This allows you to go through mediation with a clear picture of how your decisions will affect your case and your future. It also helps avoid any legal pitfalls. Even though you and your spouse may agree on a certain point, it doesn't mean that it is necessarily a wise choice or that a judge would allow it.

The mediator can draft a memorandum of agreement after the couple reaches an agreement on the disputed issues. Because mediators are not allowed to give legal advice, it is best to take this agreement to your lawyer before signing anything. You can discuss the consequences and legal ramifications of your proposed agreement with your lawyer, and if need be, have another session with the mediator to work out the kinks.

When mediation is not appropriate

There are instances in which mediation may not be a good choice for negotiating a divorce settlement. If your marriage has been subject to abuse and intimidation, the hostilities between you and your husband can impair your ability to effectively communicate your needs. Mediation is also not a good idea if there are drug or alcohol abuse issues or any mental impairment by either party.

Both parties need to feel free to express their opinions without fear of reprisal, be able to rationally discuss the issues at hand, and be willing to compromise.

Mediation can prevent court battles

While mediation may not be for everyone, it does allow you to still control the outcome of your settlement agreement. Mediation is less adversarial, time-consuming, and costly than battles waged in the courtroom. The details of your private life are kept confidential, and the emphasis is shifted from finding fault towards compromise.

Generally, mediation is a good way to settle your issues. Since both spouses contribute in mediation, they are more likely to stand by the decisions made, and also feel less resentment later on. Not all issues have to be settled in mediation, though. Couples still have the option of using court litigation or arbitration for decisions that can't be reached through mediation.

Arbitration

Arbitration is an alternative method of conflict resolution, which involves submitting your dispute to a third party for resolution. Arbitration might be considered when negotiations have broken down and certain issues can't be decided through mediation.

Arbitration as a means to settle disputes

Some divorce cases can take on a life of their own, dragging out endlessly with pre-trial hearings, discovery procedures, and delayed court dates. As bank accounts are drained, arbitration may become a viable option to settle your disputes.

Arbitration is generally less expensive and time consuming compared to a court trial, which is a plus for couples that want to get on with their lives.

Arbitration can be either binding or non-binding

Arbitration may be either binding or not. Most family law issues can be decided in arbitration, but custody and child support may not be considered binding by some court systems. Non-binding arbitration can allow a couple to see how the issues would probably be solved in the court room, thus encouraging a settlement without going to trial.

Beginning arbitration

To begin the arbitration process, an arbitrator is chosen and agreed upon by the lawyers for both sides. Most arbitrators are usually attorneys or retired judges, and knowledgeable in divorce law. The parties involved pay for arbitrators, and it is usually determined who will pay the fees before proceedings begin. You can also elect to have the arbitrator decide who will pay for the proceedings as well as the cost of representing counsel.

The process of arbitration

Arbitration is similar to a court trial without the publicity. Unless specifically requested, the proceedings are not recorded and transcribed (thereby not becoming public record).

During the proceedings, the arbitrator listens to the arguments from the lawyers for both sides. After reviewing the relevant evidence, the arbitrator then makes a decision.

Before proceedings, both parties usually sign a clause stating that they will abide by the decision. In the event of severe injustice, arbitration decisions can be appealed on the same grounds as a court judgment.

The number of issues to be resolved and what type of schedule is worked out with the spouses, their attorneys, and the arbitrator affect the amount of time that arbitration takes. Overall, arbitration is much more time efficient than court hearings.

The Divorce Trial

Tensions can run high as you and your spouse try to negotiate a divorce settlement. Feelings of frustration can become tinged with thoughts of revenge. If either side is unwilling to compromise, your case is likely to end up going to court. You may think that there is no better way to vindicate yourself than taking the matter before a judge.

Going to court should be your last resort

This is where you need to separate your emotions from the business at hand, as having your divorce case decided by a judge is not a step to be taken lightly. A court trial should be your last resort due to the time and money involved. Bank accounts can be drained rapidly with pre-trial hearings, formal discovery, court cost, and litigation fees. This is the main reason why so few divorce cases go to trial.

When deciding whether to go to trial or not, you should consider whether any prior settlement proposals are acceptable. If a proposed settlement at least meets your bottom line and is one you can live with, your lawyer may advise that you take it. If the estimated cost of a trial is more than what you stand to gain, is it really worth going to trial?

If the battle is for custody of the children, have you and your spouse discussed all viable options? Child custody battles are extremely hard on the children, and can shred any chance of being civil to one another after it is all said and done.

Try to settle as many issues as possible out of the courtroom

If your case must go to trial, try to settle as many of the issues beforehand as possible. Try to work out the majority of your differences first with the help of your lawyer, through mediation, or other forms of negotiation. This frees up the judge to concentrate only on the issues at hand. The more issues that the judge has to decide; the more likely it will be that both sides will be disappointed.

Make sure that you are adequately represented

If your divorce case is destined to go to trial, you need a lawyer to represent you. Don't even try to do this on your own. This is because court proceedings are based on the adversarial system.

By its nature, you and your spouse will be pitted against one another in the courtroom and you will need a lawyer who is well versed in divorce litigation. If your divorce is based on fault, evidence will be presented to prove the fault. All the accusations and dirty laundry that are aired in the courtroom become public record.

Be prepared to go to trial

You need to be prepared to have your case heard by a judge. Your lawyer should go over how the trial will likely proceed and help you practice for any questions that may come up.

Be totally honest with your lawyer about what has happened in your marriage, whether it makes you look bad or not. Your lawyer needs to be prepared before you go to trial, without being surprised by something that opposing counsel brings up in the courtroom. During the trial, you should try to remain calm and present a professional appearance. Emotional outbursts don't help your case.

Pre-trial hearings

Before the trial actually starts, there may be pre-trial hearings to help narrow down the issues that will be decided by the court. These meetings will include the judge, both spouses, and their lawyers. Sometimes couples can reach an agreement during these pre-trial hearings. If no agreement is reached at this stage, the case goes to trial. In a divorce trial, a judge, not a jury, makes the final decision in your case.

The divorce trial

When your divorce trial begins, the attorneys for both sides will make their opening statements. This outlines what is being sought and the reasons why. The next stage involves examination of the issues by the lawyers. Your lawyer will ask you questions that support your case. Your spouse's lawyer is then given the opportunity to cross-examine you.

Expect to be put on the hot seat. It is the opposing lawyer's job to prove that you are in the wrong, and any of your past mistakes are fair game. It is always best to answer all questions directly and honestly.

After your spouse has gone through the same process, the lawyers for both sides will call any witnesses that reinforce their positions. These can be counselors, child custody evaluators, friends, and business associates. They can also present any relevant documentation to help prove their case.

Closing arguments and the judge's ruling

The next step involves the closing arguments. The lawyers for both sides review the basis for their client's claims, interpreting the facts as substantiated by the evidence. This is the lawyer's last chance to sway the judge's decision.

After closing arguments, the judge will usually rule. If the judge needs more time to review the case, the matter may be taken "under advisement" to be decided at a later date (usually within two months). Once the ruling is established, it is incorporated into your divorce decree, along with any non-litigated agreements, and the divorce is finalized.

Appealing the judge's ruling

If the outcome of your divorce trial is lopsided and unjust, you have the option of appealing the verdict. Be warned that this only prolongs the process, and there is no guarantee that an appeal will be granted.

If it is established that your case was decided by a wrong interpretation of the law, you can have it reviewed by a higher court. If legal error is found, or if the judge overstepped his or her boundaries, the ruling may be overturned and the case retried.

If you are successful in your appeal, you will have to go through the whole trial process again, along with the added expense and time.

VI
Splitting the Assets and Debts

Marital vs. Separate Property

When dividing assets and debts in a divorce, it is relevant whether the item in question is considered marital property or separate property. Separate property falls under the following categories:
- Property or debt owned prior to the marriage
- Property bought during the marriage with funds owned prior to the marriage
- Gifts or inheritances
- Gifts from the other spouse
- Assets or debts acquired after separation

Equitable distribution states also take into consideration property acquired during the marriage if it is titled in just one spouse's name. Even if a certain item was owned prior to the marriage, some of it's value may be considered community property if:
- The value increased during the marriage.
- Joint funds were used to improve the property.
- The other spouse physically contributed in improving or repairing the property.

To claim an interest in non-marital property, you will need documentation to support your claim. This includes cancelled checks, receipts, and bank statements.

Community Property vs. Equitable Distribution

When negotiating your divorce settlement, it will be relevant whether you live in a community property state or an equitable distribution state. The following states are considered community property states:

- Arizona
- California
- Idaho
- Louisiana
- Nevada
- New Mexico
- Texas
- Washington
- Wisconsin
- Puerto Rico

Dividing assets and debts in community property states

In community property states, assets and debts acquired during the marriage are considered belonging to both spouses. Everything is basically split 50-50 regardless of how much each spouse contributed. This applies to both assets and debts.

For example, if one spouse started a business during the marriage, the other spouse would be entitled to half of its value in the divorce settlement. This spouse would also be equally liable for any debts or taxes owed on the business. In community property states, pension plans and social security benefits accumulated during the marriage can also be divided.

Factors for consideration in equitable distribution states

In equitable distribution states, settlement agreements are affected by the following factors:
- The person whose name is on the title
- The presence of any premarital agreements
- Length of the marriage
- Income, occupation, and future earning capacity of each spouse
- Economic circumstances, debts, and pensions
- Determination of fault in the divorce

Equitable distribution focuses on fair distribution as opposed to equal distribution. If your case goes to trial, a judge may opt for equal distribution if you had a long-term marriage, if both parties had relatively equal financial standings prior to marriage, if both spouses are capable of working, and if there are no minor children at home.

In other situations, a judge may award a spouse a larger settlement if that spouse:

- Has less earning capabilities
- Has made less of a financial contribution in the marriage
- Has health problems or other debilitating circumstances
- Has custody of the minor children

These are general guidelines that a court will apply when considering division in a settlement dispute. This doesn't mean that you and your spouse can't do things differently. If a settlement agreement is reached out of court, most judges will approve it.

You can check out a basic overview of property division considerations by individual states in the following table.

Property Division Factors by State

State	Community Property State	Only Marital Property Divided	Statutory List of Factors	Non-monetary (Homemaker) Contributions	Spouses Contribution to Other Spouse's Education	Economic Misconduct Considered
AL		x		x	x	
AK	x		x	x		x
AZ	x				x	x
AR		x	x	x		
CA	x		x	x	x	x
CO		x	x	x		x
CT			X	x	x	x
DE			x	x	x	x
DC		X	x	x		x
FL		x	x	x	x	x
GA		x				
HI			x	x		
ID	x		x			
IL		x	x	x		
IN		x	x	x	x	x
IA			X	x	x	x
KS			x			
KY		x	x	x	x	x
LA	x					

State	Community Property State	Only Marital Property Divided	Statutory List of Factors	Non-monetary (Homemaker) Contributions	Spouses Contribution to Other Spouse's Education	Economic Misconduct Considered
ME		x	x	x		
MD		x	x	x		
MA			x	x	x	x
MI		x		x	x	x
MN		x	x	x		
MS		x		x	x	x
MO		x	x	x	x	x
MT			x	x		x
NE		x		x		
NV	x	x		x	x	x
NH				x	x	x
NJ		x	x	x	x	x
NM	x					
NY		x	x	x	x	x
NC		x	x	x	x	x
ND				x	x	x
OH		x	x	x	x	x
OK		x		x		x
OR				x	x	x
PA		x	x	x	x	x
RI		x	x	x	x	x
SC		x	x	x	x	x
SD				x		x
TN		x	x	x	x	x
TX	x					x
UT						
VT			x	x	x	x
VA		x	x	x	x	x
WA	x		x			
WV		x	x	x	x	x
WI	x	x	x	x	x	x
WY		x	x	x		

The Family Home

Many times, one of the biggest assets a couple has is the family home. Deciding how to split this asset can become emotionally charged because each spouse may feel an attachment to the home, due to the effort and money put into it. Below are some options on handling the family home.

<u>Option one: one spouse keeps the home</u>

This is a common arrangement, which allows the minor children to continue living in the family home. Some judges will also make this determination should your case go to trial.

Generally, the spouse that retains the house is responsible for the mortgage payments, taxes, insurance, and upkeep of the house. The other spouse can receive a cash settlement, other property, or less debt in exchange for his or her equity in the property.

The spouse that moves out can sign a quitclaim deed relinquishing his or her right to the property, and should also try to get the other spouse to refinance the mortgage. The reason for this is that most mortgages are in both spouse's names, and should one fail to pay, the mortgage company will hold the other spouse liable. This can come as an unpleasant surprise many years later, especially if you hold no interest in the house.

One way around this is to have a provision added to the settlement agreement stating that the nonresidential spouse is held harmless should the other spouse default on the mortgage. What this means is that the spouse who has moved out can sue the other spouse for the amount due. If the court orders the house to be sold to satisfy a judgment, then the nonresidential spouse can be paid back any lost funds out of the net profit.

<u>Option Two: each spouse retains an interest in the home</u>

Sometimes the spouse that moves out can retain an interest in the house until it is sold. This situation needs to be entered into carefully, as the residential spouse has some control over when and how much the other spouse is paid. The house can go into disrepair or become stale on the market, meaning it sells for less than it would have at the time of the divorce.

If the home would make a good rental property, this is an option for spouses who can continue to work together. You can have a real estate company manage the property, make the mortgage payments, and split the proceeds for you. You will need to consult with your tax advisor about the implications of being joint landlords.

Option Three: the house is sold and the proceeds split

In some situations, it may make more sense to sell the house and split the profits. This may be the case if neither spouse can afford to live there on just one income, if the house holds bad memories, or if neither spouse wants to remain in the house. If this is the case, it may be easiest to sell the house before the divorce is finalized.

If it will take some time to sell the house, it can be sold after the divorce and the proceeds split at that time, minus any closing costs. If you and your spouse do choose to sell the home, consider adding a clause in your settlement agreement outlining how the tax consequences will be handled.

If each spouse claims "use of residence," both will be entitled to half of the "sale of the residential home exclusion." If you are considering selling the family home, you should talk with your accountant about the tax implications.

Pensions and Retirement Accounts

Many people forget about retirement assets when dividing the marital estate, without realizing how valuable they are. Pensions are considered marital property even if just one spouse earned the pension. The amount earned during the marriage is divisible, while any amount earned prior to the marriage and after the date of separation is considered separate property.

While you may not want a portion of your husband's pension, you can use it as a bargaining tool in settlement negotiations. You can take cash payment now in exchange for your husband keeping the entire pension at the time of retirement. You may also choose to divide the pension.

Qualified Domestic Relations Orders

Dividing pensions from private employers requires a court order called a "Qualified Domestic Relations Order" or QDRO. This is a court order that names someone other than the plan holder to receive payments from the plan. For military and certain types of government pensions, different orders are required.

It is your lawyer's responsibility to prepare the QDRO. If these orders are not prepared according to the individual plan specifications, the company paying the pension will not honor them. QDRO's need to be submitted when you file for the divorce, and settled before the divorce is finalized.

A QDRO can specify when the non-pension spouse receives his or her portion of the proceeds. Proceeds may be awarded as a lump sum (if the pension plan allows it), or may be paid out at the time of retirement.

Pensions options

If the non-pension spouse decides not to cash out his or her portion of the benefits, but chooses to keep it until retirement, that portion stops growing once the divorce is finalized. The non-pension spouse will then be responsible for the taxes on his or her share when the money is received.

Provisions may also be added for survivor's benefits if the plan's owner dies prematurely. There can also be a stipulation that benefits will be paid to the ex-spouse if alimony payments are delinquent.

Pension valuations

You can hire an actuary to appraise the pension's worth, or you can contact the plan's administrator and request a current value of the plan. Valuations are based on the time of separation, not when the divorce is finalized, and worth is determined by the future value.

Other retirement plans

Individual retirement accounts (IRA's), and simplified employee pensions (SEP's) don't require a QDRO to be divided, but it is advisable. If the division is not worded correctly and handled properly, there can be substantial tax consequences. If you transfer part of your IRA to your spouse as part of the divorce agreement, there should be not any tax cost to either of you.

The value of the IRA can also be split at the time of the divorce if it is rolled over into an ex-spouse's IRA (which must occur within 60 days of the withdrawal). Conversely, if you withdraw half of the money from your IRA to give to your spouse as a cash settlement, you will be subject to a 10% penalty if the withdrawal is done before you are 59 ½.

Payments

Couples may choose to delay payout until the time of retirement, at which time payments are made to both spouses. The non-pensioned spouse can also elect to receive periodic payments (at least one per year) under Section 72(t) of the tax code. Payments must take place over a 5-year period or until the account owner is 59 1/2, whichever is longer. Once this period is up, the payment amount can be adjusted.

Withdrawal penalties

If the withdrawal is in direct relation to the divorce decree, there should be no early withdrawal penalty, but the money will still be taxed as income. Your settlement agreement will require specific wording to avoid the early withdrawal penalty.

If the IRA owner withdraws the cash as a direct payment without a QDRO, then he or she will be assessed the early withdrawal penalty, not the spouse that receives the cash.

Annuities

Annuities require a QDRO in order to be divided, and should be handled in conjunction with the plan's administrator. Funds received from an annuity can be kept in a separate annuity should the receiving spouse chose not to rollover the funds into an IRA.

An important consideration with annuities is to change the plan's beneficiary should you die. If you no longer wish your spouse to be the beneficiary, you will need to have this changed.

Consult your financial planner

While retirement accounts may be one of the biggest marital assets, splitting them up should not be taken lightly. Because tax legislation is ever changing, it is best to have a tax consultant or financial planner explain the various options and help draw up the papers.

Business Assets and Professional Degrees

It is more common these days to consider a professional degree that was earned during the marriage as part of the marital estate. If you worked while your husband attended school to receive an advanced degree, you may be entitled to some of the value of that degree.

Determining the value of a professional degree

It's important to note that if the degree has not yet been earned it has no value. This is because there is no guarantee that the education will be continued after the divorce. To determine the value of a professional degree or career, your lawyer will probably consult an evaluator to help assign a value of the potential earning due to the degree.

Determining the value of a business

If either you or your husband has ownership in a business, it is important to also assign a value to it. If your business is very small (earning less than $25,000 per year), you may be able to reach an agreement with your spouse on its value without having an outside appraisal.

For a larger business, you will probably need to seek a professional evaluation. Talk with your CPA for a referral or check the yellow pages for a qualified appraiser. Your business appraiser will need the following information to begin the evaluation, in addition to other specific documents that he or she may request.

The name of Business _____

Physical Address _____

Type of business _____

Date business was established or bought

_____

Was the business purchased prior to your marriage?

_____

Was the business gifted?

_____

Was the business bought?

_____

What was the purchase price?

_____

Was the business built from the ground up?

_____

What were the start-up costs?

_____

_____

What is your involvement in the business?

_____

_____

What is your spouses' involvement in the business?

_____

_____

What is the structure of the business (i.e., sole proprietorship, partnership, a corporation, etc.)?

_____

What property is owned by the business?

_____

_____

You will also need copies of the following information:

- Federal and state tax returns for the last five years.
- Financial statements for the last five years.
- Business assets and inventory
- Business debts and liabilities
- Stock certificates, list of shareholders and their number of shares
- Past loan applications - to show income basis
- Past purchase offers - to show a prior established value

Next to real estate, a business may be one of the most valuable assets a couple owns; therefore, it is important to determine its fair value. Once a value has been determined, this information can be used in dividing the assets and debts.

Asset Worksheets

This section is quite large and may take a while to fill out. Going through a divorce will probably give you a better grasp of your financial situation than at any other time in your life.

Not all the information may be applicable in your situation, so just fill in the sections that apply. When filling in the following information, you will notice spaces for equity or value held jointly, in your name only, and in your spouse's name only.

<u>Separate vs. marital property</u>

If the item was purchased prior to marriage, put the value under your name only or your husband's name only accordingly. If the asset was a gift during your marriage, also put the value under whoever received the gift. If the asset was purchased during your marriage, put it under equity or value held jointly.

<u>Find out where you stand financially</u>

It may seem petty going into such detail, but many well-intentioned spouses end up getting the shaft by trying to get the whole thing over with quickly. How the assets and debts are split does make a difference when you are struggling to survive after your divorce.

Take the time now to find out where you stand financially. You'll thank yourself later on. The following worksheets will help you to see how the books balance out in the end.

Real Estate: Include family home, vacation properties, rental property, land, timeshares, etc.

Address	Date of Purchase	Purchased Prior to marriage?	Purchase Price	Current Value	Equity Held Jointly	Equity in your name	Equity in your spouse's name
Additional real estate can be listed on a separate sheet with the total values listed here under joint equity, your equity, and spouse's equity.							

Totals: $_____ $_____ $_____

Vehicles: Cars, trucks, motorcycles, RV's, boats, airplanes, etc.

Make Model Serial # License	Year	Date of Purchase	Purchased Prior to Marriage?	Loan Balance	Equity Held Jointly	Equity in your name	Equity in spouses' name
Additional vehicles can be listed on a separate sheet with the total values listed here under joint equity, your equity, and your spouse's equity.							

Totals: $_____ $_____ $_____

Checking Accounts: Personal, business, children's, etc.

Bank Name & Address	Account Number	Held prior to marriage?	Current Balance Held Jointly	Current Balance in Your Name Only	Current Balance in Spouse's Name Only
Additional accounts can be listed on a separate sheet with the total values listed here under joint balance, your balance, and your spouse's balance.					

Totals: $_____ $_____ $_____

Savings Accounts: Personal, business, children's, etc.

Bank Name & Address	Account Number	Held prior to marriage?	Current Balance Held Jointly	Current Balance in Your Name Only	Current Balance in Spouse's Name Only
Additional accounts can be listed on a separate sheet with the total values listed here under joint balance, your balance, and your spouse's balance.					

Totals:　　$_____　$_____　$_____

Certificates of Deposit:

Bank Name & Address	Account Number	Held prior to marriage?	Current Balance Held Jointly	Current Balance in Your Name Only	Current Balance in Spouse's Name Only
Additional CD's can be listed on a separate sheet with the total values listed here under joint balance, your balance only, or your spouse's balance only.					

Totals:　　$_____　$_____　$_____

Mutual Funds and Money Market Accounts:

Institution Name & Address	Account Number	Held prior to marriage?	Current Balance Held Jointly	Current Balance in Your Name Only	Current Balance in Spouse's Name Only
Additional accounts can be listed on a separate sheet with total values listed here under joint balance, your balance only, or your spouse's balance only.					

Totals:　　$_____　$_____　$_____

Stocks and Options:

Company	Bought Prior to Marriage	Date of Purchase	Purchase Price	# Of Stocks Owned	Current Value Held Jointly	Current Value in Your Name Only	Current Value in Spouse's Name
Additional stocks can be listed on a separate sheet with total values listed here under joint value, your value only, or your spouse's value only.							

Totals: $_____ $_____ $_____

Bonds: Corporate, municipal, tax-exempt, US savings, etc.

Bond Type	Bought Prior to Marriage	Date Bought	Purchase Price	Quantity and Maturity Date	Current Value Held Jointly	Current Value in Your Name Only	Current Value in Spouse's Name
Additional bonds can be listed on a separate sheet with total values listed here under joint value, your value only, or your spouse's value only.							

Totals: $_____ $_____ $_____

Annuities and Trusts:

Company	Purchased Prior to Marriage or Inherited?	Date of Purchase or Inheritance and Name of Beneficiary	Purchase Price	Current Value Held Jointly	Current Value Held in Your Name Only	Current Value Held in Your Spouse's Name
Additional annuities and trusts can be listed on a separate sheet with total values listed here under joint value, your value only, or your spouse's value only.						

Totals: $_____ $_____ $_____

Whole Life Insurance Policies:

Company	Policy #	Beneficiary	Cash Surrender Value of Policy in Your Name	Cash Surrender Value of Policy in Your Spouse's Name
Additional policies can be listed on a separate sheet with total values listed here under your value only, or your spouse's value only.				

Totals: $_____ $_____ $_____

Retirement: Pension, IRA's, SEP's, 401K, etc.

Type	Where Held	Date Initiated	Current Value in your Name	Current Value in your Spouse's Name
Additional retirement accounts can be listed on a separate sheet with total values listed here under your value only, or your spouse's value only.				

Totals: $_____ $_____ $_____

Collections: Art, jewelry, coins, collectibles, furs, etc.

Description	Date Bought	Purchase Price	Current Value	Net value held jointly	Net value in your name only	Net value in spouses' name only
Additional collections can be listed on a separate sheet with total values listed here under joint value, your value only, or your spouse's value only.						

Totals: $_____ $_____ $_____

Personal Injury Awards/Pending Litigation:

Date Awarded or information from pending case	Terms of Judgment or damages sought	Value of Judgment in Both of Your Names	Value of Judgment in Your Name Only	Value of Judgment in Your Spouse's Name Only

Totals: $_____ $_____ $_____

Other Financial Assets:

1. **Treasury Bonds and Bills** _____
2. **Commodities and Futures**_____
3. **Oil and Mineral Leases**_____
4. **Offshore Bank Accounts**_____

5. **College Funds - Value and Recipient:**
    - a. _____
    - b. _____
6. **Safety Deposit Boxes (take pictures)- contents:**
    - c. _____
    - d. _____
    - e. _____
    - f. _____
    - g. _____
    - h. _____
    - i. _____
7. **Other:** _____

Household, Shop, and Outdoor Items

While it may seem silly to list everything, when you have to replace all the items below, it can add up to quite a bit. Even if your spouse ends up taking everything, you should still be compensated for the approximate value.

Household Items:

Item	Approximate Value		
	Acquired jointly during marriage	**Owned by self prior to marriage Or gifted during marriage**	**Owned by spouse prior to marriage Or gifted during marriage**
Dining Room Set			
Couch			
Chairs			
Coffee and End Table			
TV's (Describe)	1._____ 2._____ 3._____	1._____ 2._____ 3._____	1._____ 2._____ 3._____
TV's (Describe)	1._____ 2._____ 3._____	1._____ 2._____ 3._____	1._____ 2._____ 3._____
Stereo Equipment			
VCR/ DVD			
Pictures/ Paintings (describe)	1._____ 2._____ 3._____ 4._____ 5._____ 6._____	1._____ 2._____ 3._____ 4._____ 5._____ 6._____	1._____ 2._____ 3._____ 4._____ 5._____ 6._____

Item	Approximate Value		
	Acquired jointly during marriage	**Owned by self prior to marriage Or gifted during marriage**	**Owned by spouse prior to marriage Or gifted during marriage**
Bedroom Sets: (Describe)	1. _____ 2. _____ 3. _____	1. _____ 2. _____ 3. _____	1. _____ 2. _____ 3. _____
Desks			
Computers			
China			
Silver			
Crystal			
Cameras Camcorder			
Stove			
Refrigerator			
Microwave			
Freezer			
China Cabinet			
Washer			
Dryer			
Hope Chest			
Musical Instruments			
Guns			
Vacuum Cleaner			
Carpet Cleaner			
Office Equipment			
Game Systems			
Billiard Table			
Other:			

Totals: $_____ $_____ $_____

Outdoor and Shop Equipment:

Item	Approximate Value		
	Purchased jointly during marriage	**Owned by self prior to marriage Or gifted during marriage**	**Owned by spouse prior to marriage Or gifted during marriage**
Yard Tractor			
Lawn Mower			
Weed Eater			

Item	Approximate Value		
	Purchased jointly during marriage	**Owned by self prior to marriage Or gifted during marriage**	**Owned by spouse prior to marriage Or gifted during marriage**
Ladders			
Drills			
Hand Tools			
Table Saw			
Other Shop Tools			
Tool Chests			
Snow Blower/ Snow Plow			
Bicycles			
Tents and Camping Equipment			
Ski Equipment			
Grill			
Patio Furniture			

Totals:　　$_____　$_____　$_____

Asset Totals

Type of Asset	Joint Value	Your Value	Your Spouse's Value
Real Estate			
Vehicles			
Checking Accounts			
Savings Accounts			
CD's			
Mutual Funds & Money Market Accounts			
Stocks & Options			
Bonds			
Annuities & Trusts			
Life Insurance Cash Value			
Retirement Plans			
Collections			
Awards & Pending Litigation			
Business Assets			
Other Investments			
Household Items			
Shop and Outdoor Items			
Other Assets			

Totals: $_____ $_____ $_____

Debt Worksheet

Type and Acct Information	Source Of Debt	% Rate	Loan amt & monthly payment in both names	Loan amt & monthly payment for you	Loan amt & monthly payment for your spouse
Bank Loans					
1.					
2.					
3.					
4.					
Home Equity Loans					
1.					
2.					
Finance Company Loans					
1.					
2.					
3.					
4.					
Vehicle Loans					
1.					
2.					
College Loans					
1.					
2.					
Mortgage Loans					
1.					
2.					
3.					

Type and Acct Information	Source Of Debt	% Rate	Loan amt & monthly payment in both names	Loan amt & monthly payment for you	Loan amt & monthly payment for your spouse
Credit Cards					
1.					
2.					
3.					
4.					
5.					
6.					
7.					
Liens Judgments Collection Accounts					
1.					
2.					
3.					
4.					
Private Loans					

Totals: $_____ $_____ $_____

Carry these totals below to get a clear view of the debt situation.

Here are other potential debts that you need to take into consideration:

Type of Debt	In Both Names	In Your Name	In Your Spouse's Name
Doctors			
Dentists			
Attorneys			
Accountants			
Federal Taxes			
State Taxes			
Property Taxes			
Stocks purchased on margin			
Sales Contracts			

Totals: $_____ $_____ $_____

Total Debt		
In Both Names	**In Your Name**	**In Your Spouse's Name**

Total Monthly Payments		
In Both Names	**In Your Name**	**In Your Spouse's Name**

Dividing Assets and Debts

Now it's time to start deciding how everything will be split. The guidelines discussed in the section on community property states vs. equitable distribution states are general rules that judges use to split the assets and debts in a divorce trial. If your case does go to trial, it will also be relevant whether your divorce is based on fault or not.

It's not necessary to have your settlement decided by a judge, though. You can save a lot of time and expense by reaching your settlement out of court. As long as your settlement is reasonable, most judges will approve it.

Cash is king

When you begin to divide your assets, remember that cash is king. A settlement that includes a lump sum payment is preferable to receiving assets that will depreciate, or payments that may disappear after the divorce is finalized.

Consider the tax consequences

Talking with a financial planner about how assets and debts should be split can save you a lot of headaches and expense later on. If you will be receiving property, you need to consider any capital gains tax that you will have to pay if the property is sold at a later date. The potential tax from a subsequent sale will lower the value of the property.

There are also tax consequences to consider when dividing stocks and bonds. If the stocks or bonds are transferred before the divorce is finalized, it will be considered a transfer between spouses and should be tax exempt.

Transfers occurring after the divorce will fall under the same tax rules as transfers between unrelated people, unless it is stated specifically in your settlement agreement that these transfers will occur within six years and are related to the end of the marriage.

Finding out where you stand

The best place to start dividing assets and debts is to look at the whole picture. Bring the totals forward from your previous worksheet pages and list below. You can get a tentative net value for each category (sole or joint) by subtracting the debts from the assets.

	Joint Value	Value in Your Name	Value in Your Spouse's Name
Assets			
Debts			
Net			

If there is a huge discrepancy between your net worth and your spouse's net worth, this is where joint net worth can come into play. Assets can be shifted to the spouse who has a lesser net worth, or debts to the spouse who has a greater net worth to even things out.

Relative value of assets and debts

Also, keep in mind the relative value of the assets and debts. An equal value of shares in junk bonds and blue chip stocks will not stay equal over the long run. A high interest rate loan that has the same balance as a low interest rate loan will actually cost you more money over time. Loans need to be figured as if they will be paid out over time to get the true value.

Considerations for debts that your husband assumes

Another thing to consider when splitting debts is that your divorce decree will not release you from previous agreements with your creditors. If your husband defaults on a joint loan that he assumed in the divorce, the creditors will then expect you to pay off the loan. With this in mind, you can try to have your husband refinance the loans solely into his own name.

If it seems unlikely that your spouse will refinance, you should get some type of security or collateral to insure that proper payments are made. You can include a clause in your divorce agreement that allows you to hold the title to certain personal property of your husband until the debt is paid off. If the loan then goes into default, you can seize the property to pay off the loan.

Protect yourself

Always try to protect your future when dividing your assets and debts. Your husband's promises to make payments to you or to pay off certain debts can end up being empty promises in the near future. Assets have a way of disappearing, payments become past due, and creditors begin to call when payments are missed. Approach your settlement looking at the worse case scenario and negotiate accordingly.

How Bankruptcy Affects Divorce

It's common today for most married couples to live paycheck to paycheck. When such couples divorce, their financial standing is shaken due to their reduced resources and the added expenses that go along with divorce.

Financial reality

After a divorce, getting by on just one paycheck can become a real strain, if not totally impossible. This can eventually push people to declare bankruptcy just in order to survive. The possibility of a future bankruptcy should be kept in mind as you begin to draft your settlement agreement.

You can be held responsible for joint debts

If your spouse assumes some of the joint debts in the divorce settlement and then ends up declaring bankruptcy, the creditors will look to you to pay off the remaining debt. In community property states, all of the community property that you and your spouse had will be considered part of the bankruptcy estate, whether you file bankruptcy jointly or not.

In such a case, your spouse's property will be used first to settle the debt, followed by nonexempt community property. As you can see, you need to consider the implications of a future bankruptcy when you divorce.

If your spouse still owes you money

If your spouse declares bankruptcy after the divorce and still owes you money or property from the divorce settlement, you might end up losing it in the bankruptcy proceedings. If your spouse does not have enough money for basic living expenses, then all or a portion of what is owed you from the divorce settlement may be discharged.

This is because the bankruptcy court will consider you a creditor in the suit. Bankruptcy courts cannot discharge child support obligations or back alimony, though.

Precautions if you think your spouse may declare bankruptcy

If it seems likely that your spouse will declare bankruptcy in the future, it may be a good idea to have the monetary payments of your divorce agreement worded as support payments (as compared to a property settlement). You'll have to pay taxes, as it is considered income, but you stand a better chance of receiving the money if your spouse does declare bankruptcy.

Protecting yourself against your spouse's future bankruptcy

You can always add a clause in your divorce agreement stating that if either spouse declares bankruptcy within three years of the divorce, he or she will be obligated to notify the other spouse 21 days prior to filing for bankruptcy. The spouse being notified can then have the option of participating in the bankruptcy case.

You can request that your spouse remain liable for the joint debts that he or she assumed after the divorce. This can help relieve the pressure of being solely responsible for these debts after the bankruptcy.

You can also protect yourself by taking a lien out on some of your spouse's property until the settlement is paid off. If your spouse then declares bankruptcy, you can seize the property in lieu of the payment you were to receive. Another option is to include a clause in your settlement agreement that child support and alimony can be increased should your spouse declare bankruptcy.

Bankruptcy before the divorce is finalized

So what happens if you or your spouse begins bankruptcy proceedings before the divorce is finalized? It is important to note that your divorce proceedings will come to a halt until the bankruptcy is resolved. It's aggravating, but it makes sense. Your settlement agreement will be no good until everything is decided in the bankruptcy process.

If you are very intent on ending your marriage, you might consider a bifurcated divorce before the bankruptcy is completed. This dissolves the legal marriage and allows you to work out the settlement agreement on property, support, and custody once the bankruptcy proceedings are finalized.

If your spouse starts bankruptcy proceedings before the divorce is finalized, you might also consider filing bankruptcy jointly, especially if the majority of the debts are held jointly. Because creditors are not parties to a divorce agreement, you will still be held liable for the debts even if your spouse is the only one declaring bankruptcy. By filing jointly, you can save a lot of headaches in figuring out how debts will be allocated in the settlement agreement, and save bad feelings afterwards.

Bankruptcy should be considered as a last resort

As a word of caution, bankruptcy proceedings are not to be taken lightly. Bankruptcy stays on your credit record from seven to ten years and will affect your ability to get credit or buy a home during this time. If you are considering bankruptcy, it is wise to consult with a certified financial planner or bankruptcy lawyer before you do. It isn't always the best solution to your debt problems.

VII
Making Decisions About the Children

Deciding Child Custody

When child custody is determined, it outlines the rights and obligations of both parents concerning their children during a separation or divorce. Because a divorce can sometimes take months to be finalized, temporary custody orders can be granted until a final custody decision is made. These orders state whom the children will live with and the visitation rights of the other parent.

Establishing temporary custody

It is common to also establish temporary support orders to assure that the children are adequately provided for. Either parent can file for temporary custody, but it is usually granted to the parent residing in the family home as a way to maintain stability in the children's lives.

If you are initiating the divorce and want temporary custody of the children, you should have your lawyer file the necessary paperwork. If your husband has served you with divorce papers but didn't file for temporary custody, then you should file your request for temporary custody as soon as possible (if you want the children to live with you during the divorce proceedings).

The ruling of temporary custody will usually remain in effect until the divorce is finalized or the court determines custody. Even though temporary custody arrangements can have some bearing on the final custody arrangements, it should not be taken for granted that the custody arrangements will remain the same.

Think of the children first

Ideally, custody decisions should be based on what is best for the children, not the needs and wants of the parents. This can be difficult sometimes, especially when the issue of custody is viewed as another win or lose proposition in your divorce case.

Suing for custody in order to get revenge or gain leverage in the divorce is horrendous. It is the children who are hurt the most in a custody battle. Divorce is very traumatic to children because they have no control over what is happening. Try to put your children's feelings first.

You will always have a connection with the other parent

When you have children, it is important to remember that divorce will not end your relationship with their father. You will still need to communicate and work with the other parent throughout your children's lives.

It may be hard, but try to encourage your children's relationship with their father. Don't berate your husband, engage in fights in front of the children, or deny visitation. If your custody battle does go to court, such dirty tricks will count against you. Try to remain civil and put your children's needs first. You can lessen the confusion and upheaval by not including your children in your divorce battle.

Courts encourage the involvement of both parents

Generally, the best custody arrangement is one that allows children access to both of the parents. Because of this, many states now lean toward joint legal custody. The most common arrangement is for one parent to have primary physical custody while the other parent receives ample visitation rights. Courts are reluctant to deny visitation to a parent unless there is evidence of physical or sexual misconduct.

Motherhood does not guarantee custody

It can no longer be assumed that custody will automatically be awarded to the mother should the matter be decided by a judge. In most states, both the mother and father have an equal right to custody of their children. Courts base custody decisions on the best interest of the child and which parent will do the best job of raising the child.

Custody doesn't have to be decided by a judge

Parents shouldn't have to go to court to decide custody because they are the ultimate experts on their children's best interests. Unfortunately, some spouses can't reach a mutual agreement on custody and the court must make the decision.

Before you automatically take this route, realize that child custody litigation is both expensive and lengthy. Many times the children are caught in a no-man's land where they are used as pawns during the ensuing custody battle.

Before you go to court, consider using a mediator skilled in child custody cases. Sometimes a mediator can help couples reach an agreement that is satisfactory to both sides. If your custody case does end up going to court, make sure that a lawyer skilled in custody litigation represents you.

Continuing jurisdiction by the court

Once custody is determined, you need to realize that the court will retain continuing jurisdiction over your divorce case until your children reach the age of majority (usually 18 or 21). This means that a petition for a change of custody can be filed after the divorce is finalized due to a change in circumstances. Once again, the "best interest of the child(ren)" will need to be taken into consideration.

Whether or not your case goes to trial, it is beneficial to consider the "best interests of the child," and put your child's needs foremost.

Types of Custody

Physical vs. legal custody

The determination of custody affects the structure of your child's life and is decided on two levels, physical and legal custody. Physical custody determines where the child will physically live. Legal custody determines who will make the major decisions that will affect the child's life such as education, religion, and medical care.

Primary physical custodian

Courts usually designate only one parent as the primary physical custodian. The custodial parent is responsible for the day-to-day care and nurturing of the child, while the non-custodial parent has the opportunity to spend time with the child as outlined in the visitation schedule.

If a mutual agreement is reached without going to court, there can be more latitude in how physical custody is outlined. This can range from one parent having primary physical custody to the child living with each parent for relatively equal amounts of time.

Today, joint legal custody is often the standard, but is not the only custody arrangement. Custody decisions will incorporate both the determination of legal and physical custody, leading to the four following custody arrangements outlined below:

1.   **Joint Legal/Joint Physical Custody** - Both parents are responsible for making major decisions that will affect the child's life. The child will also live with each parent for a relatively equal amount of time. In some cases, this can be a confusing arrangement for the child. If you choose this type of shared custody, you need to talk with your child on a regular basis to guarantee that you are satisfying the needs of your child and not just yourself. Some experts believe that in order for equal time to work, it should be split into larger time frames, such as one or two weeks blocks, instead of splitting the week between both parents. For this to be possible, both parents need to live relatively

close to each other.

2.   **Joint Legal/Sole Physical Custody** - This is the most common arrangement in many states. The child will live with one parent while the other parent will have visitation rights. Both parents will be involved in making major decisions that affect the child. It requires continuing cooperation between parents for this arrangement to work.

3.   **Sole Legal/Joint Physical Custody** - One parent is solely responsible for the care of and decision making for the child. The child usually resides with just one parent while the other parent has visitation rights, but the child can spend varying amounts of time with each parent.

4.   **Sole Legal/Sole Physical Custody** - The child resides with the custodial parent who is solely responsible for the decisions concerning the child's life, and the other parent may or may not have visitation rights. If it is determined that the non-custodial parent is unfit or is a danger to the child, visitation rights may be suspended or required to be supervised. With supervised visitation, the non-custodial parent spends time with the child in a neutral location in the presence of another adult (sometimes a court-appointed friend of the court or a counselor).

Sole legal custody is rare

Some states automatically award joint legal custody unless there is a fear that it would be detrimental to the child. In this case, sole legal custody will be granted. Other instances in which sole legal custody may be awarded are if there is evidence of abuse, abandonment, or substance abuse.

Sole legal custody doesn't remove the other parent's rights to visitation unless the court restricts visitation. Sole legal and physical custody may also be granted if the other parent relinquishes his or her parental rights.

Working through custody issues

Many times parents will fight for custody out of the fear that they will not be able to be involved in their children's lives after the divorce. A custody trial can be avoided if there are assurances of ongoing contact and provisions for ample visitation. Sometimes a parent will seek custody out of revenge or to avoid having to pay child support. Both are horrible reasons to seek custody because they have nothing to do with what is best for the children.

If parents are unable to reach a mutual agreement, they have the option of either using mediation or taking their custody case to trial. Some states require mediation before a custody case goes to trial. Mediation often allows couples to work out a viable solution that might not be available should custody have to be decided by a judge. No matter how custody is decided, you should always consider what is best for your children.

Best Interest of the Child

When the court makes custody decisions, the "best interest of the child" is used as a basis for determining custody. Even if parents can reach a mutual agreement, it is beneficial for both parents to consider the following points. Each state uses its own standards to determine custody, but below are some general guidelines that are taken into consideration:

- **Who is the primary caretaker of the child?** Generally, the primary caretaker is favored for custody, especially if the child is under the age of eight. The basis for choosing the primary caretaker is to provide continuity in a child's life. If both parents have shared parenting responsibilities, this factor will have less weight.

- **With whom does the child prefer to live with?** The wishes of the child can be taken into consideration if he or she is of sufficient age and maturity. The child must also have a valid reason for wanting to live with one parent over the other. Generally, children under the age of seven or eight are not capable of making such a big decision. Once a child is older, his or her preference will have more weight. In Georgia and West Virginia, once a child turns fourteen, the child can choose which parent to live with.

- **The quality of the child/parent relationship.** In some families, a child spends more time with and develops a closer bond to one parent. A judge may be reluctant to remove the child from that parent so as not to cause emotional suffering.

- **The presence of a stable and established home for the child.** Considerations are given to how long the child has lived in the family home, whether it is a satisfactory environment in which to raise a child, and whether the home is in acceptable physical condition. The parent who can provide continuity by keeping the child in the family home and in the same community, school, and church may be favored. Courts aim to keep the disruption in a child's life to a minimum.

- **The presence of abusive behavior.** Mental and physical abuse will be considered not only if it is against the child, but also against any other adults or children in the household. The judge will not want to place a child in harm's way.

- **The physical and mental health of each parent.** If a child's well being will be affected by a physical or mental ailment of one of the parents, it will be taken into consideration when determining custody arrangements.

- **The physical and mental health of the child.** If the child has special needs due to a mental or physical disability, consideration is given to the parent most capable of providing for the child's needs.

- **Drug or alcohol addiction.** This behavior creates a dangerous environment for the child to live in and will be give careful consideration in a custody decision.

- **The moral fitness of both parents.** The presence of non-marital relationships that have put the child in an embarrassing or a stressful situation may be taken into consideration when deciding custody. In fact, many lawyers will advise against dating before your custody issues are resolved. Homosexual relationships can also have a big impact, with the assumption by many judges that such a relationship will have and adverse effect on the child.

- **The effort of each parent in encouraging a relationship with the other parent.** If one parent is trying to damage the relationship with the other parent or is interfering with visitation rights, a judge may consider granting custody to the parent who is suffering. This "friendly parent" issue can be a double-edged sword in cases where abuse has occurred. If the concerned parent restricts contact as a means of self-protection or protection of the child, it may be viewed as interfering with the child/parent relationship. Lawyers representing such a case need to be apprised of the situation from the very beginning.

Other custody considerations

Other factors that may be taken into consideration when determining custody is the child's age and sex, the parent's ability to provide for the child, how available the parent will be for the child, and the testimony from counselors and child custody evaluators.

For more state-specific information, review the table on the following page. Once the basis for child custody is established, the type of custody will need to be determined, either mutually or through custody trial.

Custody Factors by State

State	Statutory Guidelines	Child's Wishes	Joint Legal Custody	Cooperative Parent	Domestic Violence	Health	Guardian Ad Litem
AL	x	x	x		x		
AK	x	x	x		x		x
AZ	x	x	x	x	x	x	x
AR					x		
CA	x	x		x	x	x	x
CO	x	x	x	x	x	x	x
CT		x	x				x
DE	x	x	x		x	x	x
DC	x	x	x	x	x	x	x
FL	x	x	x	x	x	x	x
GA	x	x	x		x		x
HI	x	x	x		x		x
ID	x	x	x		x	x	
IL	x	x	x	x	x	x	x
IN	x	x	x	x	x	x	x
IA	x	x	x	x	x	x	x
KS	x	x	x	x	x	x	
KY	x	x	x	x	x	x	x
LA	x	x	x		x		
ME	x	x	x		x		x
MD		x	x	x	x	x	x
MA			x		x		x
MI	x	x	x	x	x	x	x
MN	x	x	x		x	x	x

State	Statutory Guidelines	Child's Wishes	Joint Legal Custody	Cooperative Parent	Domestic Violence	Health	Guardian Ad Litem
MS	x		x			x	x
MO	x	x	x	x	x	x	x
MT	x	x	x		x		x
NE	x	x	x		x	x	x
NV	x	x	x	x	x		x
NH	x	x	x		x		x
NJ	x	x	x	x	x	x	x
NM	x	x	x	x	x	x	x
NY		x			x		x
NC		x	x		x	x	
ND	x	x	x	x	x	x	
OH	x	x	x		x	x	x
OK	x	x	x	x	x		
OR	x	x	x	x	x		x
PA	x	x	x	x	x	x	x
RI		x	x	x	x	x	x
SC		x	x	x	x	x	x
SD		x	x	x	x		
TN	x	x	x	x	x		x
TX	x	x	x	x	x	x	x
UT	x	x	x	x			x
VT	x		x		x		x
VA	x	x	x	x	x	x	x
WA	x	x			x	x	x
WV		x	x		x		
WI	x	x	x	x	x	x	x
WY	x	x	x	x	x	x	x

Child Custody Mediation

There are instances in which an agreement on child custody just can't be reached amicably between parents. Before taking your case before a judge, consider using custody mediation. Many court systems recommend mediation before proceeding to trial due to its success in resolving conflicts.

States that require mandatory mediation

In fact, California, Maine, and New Mexico require mediation as a first step in custody litigation. Many times, parents are able to reach an agreement at this stage without having to go to trial.

Advantages of mediation

There are many advantages to mediation as compared to litigation. It can prevent the inherent frustrations that go along with a court trial, saving both time and money. Most importantly, a decision is reached mutually between the parents instead of by a judge who has no idea of the family dynamics and needs.

Because mediation is conducted outside of the court system, all the angry accusations and mudslinging do not become part of the divorce record. Parents who are able to reach a mutual agreement through mediation generally are more satisfied with the outcome because it is not viewed as a win or lose proposition.

The mediator's role

A mediator, acting as a neutral third party, guides negotiations between the parents in an effort to reach a mutually acceptable custody agreement. The mediator can either be court appointed or hired by the parents. Because mediation is not adversarial, the focus is shifted away from attacking the other parent and toward working on what is best for the children.

Parents need to approach mediation with an open mind, realizing that there can be more than one solution to the situation. A mediator can suggest different approaches that may not have been previously considered and help bring out the parent's true concerns for their children. A mediator can help parents shift their focus from the "blame game" to concentrating on what their children truly need.

Mediation in difficult cases

In cases where there has been abuse or extreme bitterness between the parents, a mediator can begin by meeting with each side separately. This allows the mediator to get input from each side that is not tainted by intimidation or anger from the other parent. The mediator can continue to work with each parent separately until some common ground is found.

At this point, the parents can begin to discuss their concerns and negotiate face to face. In order to get a balanced view of the whole situation, a mediator may also meet separately with the children to find out what their needs and wants are.

Points to consider when approaching mediation

As you approach mediation, you should consider more than one possible outcome. This gives you room to negotiate. Consider the following questions before you begin negotiation:

- What do you think your children's needs and wants are?

- What type of custody arrangement do you want?

- Why do you want this custody arrangement?

- Does your husband want physical custody and what do you think his reasons are?

- What concerns do you have with your husband's parenting abilities?

- What do you think your husband's concerns are?

- What type of visitation schedule do you think is reasonable?

- How should vacations and holidays be handled?

- What are some reasonable options to custody and visitation?

By going into mediation with an open mind and willing to negotiate, you are much more likely to reach an agreement that both of you can live with. If an agreement is reached in the mediation process, you should have your lawyer review it and discuss the implications with you before you sign the proposed agreement.

You can always request further mediation to work out the details. Even if you and your spouse cannot reach an agreement, mediation can help both of you focus on what is best for the children before going to court.

Child Custody Trial

<u>The effects of a custody trial</u>

Having child custody decided through the court system should be considered only if personal negotiations or custody mediation doesn't help reach a solution. It is common for custody battles to carry on for months and sometimes even years.

This leaves everyone's lives in limbo until the court makes a decision. For the children who are at the center of the battle, custody litigation can drag out the healing process. For the parents, it can be next to impossible to get beyond the bitterness once everything is settled.

<u>Using a custody evaluator</u>

Before you take your custody case to trial, consider hiring a private custody evaluator to review your case. Make sure that both you and your husband agree to have this done and agree on the evaluator.

The custody evaluator will interview both of the parents, the children, and any other people who are involved in the children's live. The evaluator will then make a recommendation as to where the children should live. Even if you disagree with the recommendation, realize that it is unlikely that a judge would rule differently.

<u>Elements of a custody trial</u>

If your case does go to trial, a judge will determine the custody arrangements, child support and visitation schedules. Most custody trials are closed hearings in which spectators are not allowed. The elements of a custody trial will vary by state and individual circumstances, but generally include the following:

- **<u>Pre-trial Conference</u>** - The courts will usually schedule a pre-trial conference to outline the case.

Temporary orders for custody and support may be ordered at this time if they are not already in effect. Many states will also require that both parents attend parenting classes and court ordered mediation. The judge may also order a custody evaluation and appoint a Guardian Ad Litem for the children.

- **Parenting Classes** - In some states, parenting classes are mandatory before a divorce is finalized or before a custody trial. These classes aim to educate parents about the effects of divorce and custody battles on children. The classes often outline the options that are available concerning custody and visitation and help the parents to focus on the children's needs.

- **Guardian Ad Litem** - An attorney may be retained to represent and protect the interests if the children. One or both of the parents pay for the children's attorney, which is called a guardian ad litem. The guardian ad litem will not only talk with the parents and children, but also with custody evaluators, counselors, and anyone else who has pertinent information to the case. The judge will take into consideration the recommendations of the guardian ad litem.

- **Custody Lawyers** - You will need a lawyer skilled in child custody litigation to represent you in your custody case. Your lawyer can help you prepare for the case and discuss the possible outcomes. Your lawyer will need to know everything that is relevant to your case in order to prove that you are a good parent. Be prepared to have bitter feelings toward your ex after the trial because your general character and parenting abilities will be brought into question by opposing counsel. It's the nature of the game.

- **Custody Evaluation** - It is common to have the court order a custody evaluation done by a skilled psychologist or social worker. The evaluator will meet individually with both parents and the children. The custody evaluator may also interview grandparents, babysitters, and any other people who are important in the children's lives. An evaluator may also conduct psychological tests to determine the fitness of the parents and the emotional stability and wants of the children. A custody evaluator's recommendation will be taken into consideration in the custody trial.

- **Custody Hearing** - Each side will have the opportunity to present their case, along with any substantiating evidence and witnesses. Opposing counsel is allowed to cross-examine each parent and any witnesses in order to dispute facts or make the case more clear. The judge may request a private meeting with the children in his or her chambers if they are old enough to express themselves. This allows the judge to find out the children's wishes without them being influenced by the presence of their parents.

- **The Judge's Decision** - Judges use the state's statutory laws as a basis for custody determination. A judge will also take into consideration the recommendations from mediators, custody evaluators, and the guardian ad litem. As a general rule, judges are reluctant to split up siblings and will consider what is in the "best interest" of the children. Stability for the children is often an important factor, along with the child's age and relationship with each parent. The judge will also determine a fixed visitation schedule. The visitation schedule outlines detailed dates and times for visitation in an attempt to prevent further conflict. Child support will be assessed according to state guidelines and adjusted according to the unique circumstances of your situation.

Your emotions after a custody trial

Because someone invariably loses in a court trial, it's common to harbor intense bitter feelings toward your spouse after a custody battle. It's perfectly understandable to feel this way, but you shouldn't let your emotions affect your children.

Even though it can be hard, try not to cut down your ex in front of the children. Try even harder to do what is best for the children. This means talking civilly with your husband in front of the children, and abiding by visitation schedules and support orders. When you don't, the children are the ones who are affected the most.

Other Custody Issues

Even if custody has been settled, there may be other issues that come up down the road. Below is a discussion of some of the major concerns such as parental kidnapping, death of the custodial parent, grandparent's rights, and violation of court orders.

Parental Kidnapping

In some cases where there has been a bitter custody dispute, there continues to be ongoing conflict between the parents over the children. Feelings of frustration with the justice system can spur a parent to take the children and leave the state (or even the country) without the knowledge of the other parent. Children may experience lasting effects of a parental kidnapping, and the parent who abducts the children may face criminal and civil penalties for his or her actions.

If you suspect the other parent will take the children

You should take the other parent seriously if he ever threatens to take the children. You should be prepared if you think that the possibility even exists that your ex may kidnap the children. Have a record of your ex-husband's driver's license number, social security number, credit cards, license plates, and anything else that could be used to trace his whereabouts. Also, have on hand any current photos and written descriptions of the children.

Make sure that your children have their name, phone number, and address memorized. Also teach your children how to place a collect call. Be sure to alert babysitters, school officials, and bus drivers that your husband may try to kidnap the children and how to possibly handle the situation. Nothing is worse than going to pick up your children, only to find that they have been taken without your knowledge. Be prepared for the worst.

What to do if your children are kidnapped

If your husband does abduct the children, you should immediately call the police. Explain the situation and show them the current custody orders. Also contact your lawyer to initiate proceedings for contempt of court and see about obtaining a felony warrant against your ex. Call your ex's friends, family, neighbors, and employer for any clues to his possible whereabouts.

Federal and international help in kidnapping cases

The Federal Parental Kidnapping Prevention Act requires that all states make available the Federal Parent Locator Service to track down a parent in hiding. It also requires all states to follow the standard of the Uniform Child Custody Jurisdiction Act. This act was designed to resolve interstate custody jurisdiction by requiring courts to defer to the custody orders from another state or jurisdiction.

In cases where the child is taken out of the country, the Hague Convention on the Civil Aspects of International Child Abduction can help. Participating countries will abide by the jurisdiction of the court in which the children lived when they were abducted.

If you fear that your children will be taken to another country

If the possibility exists that your husband will try to take the children to a foreign country, make sure the children's passports are in a safe place. This is because the government will not issue another passport if there is already one on file.

If your children do not have passports already, you may consider getting them now to prevent your husband from applying for their passports at a later time. If your children are kidnapped, contact the State Department to alert them that your husband may try to apply for passports.

Another idea is to file a motion with the court to deny passport privileges to the children. If these papers are forwarded to the US State Department, passports will not be issued for the children and they cannot leave the country.

Death of A Custodial Parent

Another custody issue that is not often considered is what will happen to the children if the custodial parent dies. The non-custodial parent will automatically get full custody of the children in most instances. The only way to prevent this is to have your ex terminate his parental rights.

This may be a consideration if the other parent wishes to have no contact with the children after the divorce and you would want someone else to raise your children in the event of your death. It is also a relevant issue in cases where there has been sexual abuse or extreme physical abuse against the children. If your spouse is willing to relinquish his parental rights, you need to realize that child support obligations will also be released.

Grandparents Rights

The rights of grandparents are often un-addressed when deciding custody, but all states have provisions giving grandparents the right to visit their grandchildren. Generally, the children's relationship with their grandparents is beneficial to the children and should be encouraged.

In cases where the bitterness of the divorce has caused alienation with the grandparents, grandparents may request visitation rights from the court. The courts will take into consideration the best interests of the children before ordering visitation. Visitation rights will usually be granted if there has been a healthy, nurturing relationship between the children and the grandparents.

Violation of Court Orders

What happens if one parent violates the custody agreement? Violations of the custody agreement usually center on not returning the child to the custodial parent, denying visitation to the non-custodial parent, or not paying court ordered child support.

If this happens in your case, you need to contact your attorney to see about filing contempt of court charges. If it is a support issue, contact the child support agency handling your case. Courts can impose fines or jail time for parents who are in contempt of a custody order, and sometime this can persuade a parent to comply with the custody orders in the future.

Custody Modification

Once custody decisions are made, you need to realize that they are not set in stone. Most states will allow for modification of custody. As the circumstances of a child's life change, the custody arrangements may need to be reexamined. Below are some of the circumstances in which custody can be re-evaluated:

- If there is a mutual agreement between the parents to modify the current custody arrangements.

- When an older child (usually at least 14) wishes to change the custody arrangements. A judge will evaluate whether the child is of sufficient age and capability to make the choice on sound reasoning. It is important to remember that a child's needs for each parent will change, as the child grows older.

- A judge may consider a change in custody if the custodial parent moves so far away that the non-custodial parent will be prevented from seeing the child during the school year.

- If the custodial parent marries or lives with someone who neglects, abuses, or endangers the child. This may be a basis for physical custody to be awarded to the non-custodial parent.

- Major changes in the household of either parent can also affect custody and visitation. Some instances that would require a reevaluation are the arrest of a parent for a crime, parental desertion of the child, or the child living in unfit conditions.

- Custody or visitation of a parent may be restricted or taken away if there is the evidence of drug or alcohol abuse.

- When a parent endangers a child by being physically or sexually abusive, a judge will likely change custody or restrict visitation.

- In some cases, continuing or escalating conflict between the parents may require a change from joint legal custody to sole legal custody in an attempt to reduce the amount of contact and friction between the parents.

119

Considerations for modifying custody

Many judges are reluctant to modify child custody arrangements because of the disruption it can cause in a child's life. If at some point you feel that the custody arrangements need to be reconsidered, you can hire a lawyer skilled in custody litigation to represent you.

You will need to have sound reasons for requesting the change, and should be able to demonstrate that you have the ability to provide a better environment for the child.

Visitation Overview

In most divorces involving children, one parent receives primary custody of the children, while the non-custodial parent is granted visitation rights. The term visitation often strikes a sour note with non-custodial parents because it seems to diminish the importance in their children's lives. When drafting a visitation schedule, it can be helpful to call this document a parenting schedule, giving due credit to both parents in the children's lives.

Try to keep continuity between each parent's home

The children's ability to spend time with both parents is important. They are better able to adjust to their new lives by maintaining a bond with both parents after the divorce. Ideally, there should be a sense of continuity between both houses by maintaining some of the same rules, bedtimes, discipline, and activities. This gives children a routine that they can count on and keeps them from pitting one parent against them other.

Don't try to buy your children's love

When the non-custodial parent spends the shared time in a flurry of activity trying to entertain the children, neither the children nor the parent gets a chance to relax and bond in a natural way. After a period of time, the children may come to expect all the pampering to continue.

You can't buy your children's love. Just relax and spend some unstructured quality time with the children. Most of all, your children want to know that you are there for them and that they can just be themselves around you.

Visitation and child support are separate issues

It's important for both parents to realize that visitation is not tied to child support payments. The legal system will view both as two separate issues. Not only is it wrong, but also it is illegal to withhold visitation for the nonpayment of child support. A non-custodial parent can file contempt of court charges against the parent that has interfered with visitation. Likewise, a non-custodial parent cannot justify withholding child support if he or she is denied access to the children.

Visitation enforcement

Courts cannot make a non-custodial parent spend time with his or her children. The non-custodial parent needs to realize how important continuing contact with the children is. On the other hand, a custodial parent may not seek to restrict or deny visitation between the children and the non-custodial parent. If visitation is being denied, the non-custodial parent can petition the court to enforce the visitation or parenting schedule.

Grandparents visitation

You may feel some alienation toward your in-laws when you and your spouse divorce. It is important to remember that these people are still your children's grandparents and probably hold a special place in their heart. The bond that children have with their grandparents is unique and you should encourage it (barring cases in which such involvement would be detrimental to your children).

Children may have the opportunity to see their grandparents during time spent with the non-custodial parent when they live in the same area. In situations where everyone remains on a friendly basis, arrangements can be made for the children to spend time with their grandparents for outings, vacations, and weekends.

If there is a lot of conflict and animosity present, grandparents may not get the chance to see their grandchildren on a regular basis. Grandparents have the right to visitation privileges and can seek a court order to enforce their rights. If a judge deems that it is in the best interest of the children to see their grandparents, then visitation will be ordered.

Visitation with an absent parent

In instances where one parent has been absent from the children's lives for a long amount of time, it is a good idea to reestablish contact gradually. Children can resent being forced to spend long amounts of time with a parent that they have detached from.

The length of the visits can be increased gradually over time, giving the children an opportunity to rebuild their relationship with the absent parent.

Modifying visitation

Your parenting schedule may need to be modified from time to time due to the fact that life is never static. Sometimes visitation will need to be modified because one parent moves a long distance away. If this is the case, a typical parenting schedule won't be practical. You may need to have visitation occur during longer periods of time over Christmas break, spring break, and summer vacation.

Not only do circumstances change in your life, but also so will your children's needs. As they get older, they may wish to spend more time with the other parent. You should try to work with your children on this because a conflict on this issue can alienate them. It is human nature to want what one can't have, and by not allowing adequate contact with the other parent, resentment can build up against you.

There are other more serious instances in which visitation schedules should be reexamined, such as when the custodial parent doesn't allow the non-custodial parent to see the children. A parent's conviction of a crime will also affect the visitation schedule. If a parent endangers, abuses, or exposes the children to immoral or illegal activities, then visitation and custody should be re-evaluated.

It is best if both parents can agree on the visitation modifications. If parents can't agree, they can seek the help of a mediator or request a judge's ruling to modify the visitation schedule.

Children's reaction to visitation

What are you to do if your children don't want to spend time with their other parent? You need to emphasis to the children that it is not their decision whether to see the other parent or not. Try to encourage the contact unless there is as a real danger to their well being.

What if you're the parent that the children don't want to spend time with? Ask yourself if your visitation time can be less structured in order to work around their schedule. Try to show them that their feelings are important to you and that you will try to find other ways to spend time with them.

If a sporting event is the issue, make it to the game and then take the child out to eat afterwards. When children pull away, it usually means that they have other things going on in their lives, not that they love you any less. Try to work with them instead of forcing the issue.

Expect an adjustment period after visitation with the other parent

It is also common for children to be withdrawn after returning from time spent with the other parent. A change in their routine will cause some changes in their normal behavior. They are probably reflecting on the changes to their lives and trying to get a grip on their emotions.

It's best to allow them some alone time to readjust. Try not to pressure them for information about their other parent unless they initiate the discussion.

Restricting visitation

A judge can restrict visitation or order supervised visitation if it is believed that the children's welfare is endangered by regular visitation. Supervised visitation allows a child contact with the non-custodial parent in a safe environment.

Supervised visitation occurs in the presence of a responsible third party who oversees the parent/child interaction and insures the safety of the child. Continued contact with the non-custodial parent can help children adjust to the divorce and encourage the parent to continue to build a relationship with the children.

Some instances that warrant supervised visitation are:

• If there is the threat of parental kidnapping.

• If the non-custodial parent has a history of drug or alcohol abuse.

• If there is the threat of physical, mental, or sexual abuse.

• If the parent has threatened suicide

• Conviction of a crime

A judge will not only consider the "best interest of the child," but will also determine whether unstructured visitation would endanger the child's physical, mental, or moral health. Along with supervised visitation, a judge may also order anger management, parenting classes, and counseling.

A successful visitation schedule will allow children adequate time with the non-custodial parent. It is best to work out a schedule amicably with your spouse. If you can't communicate on friendly terms, it may be reasonable to follow a court-ordered or fixed schedule.

Visitation Schedules

<u>Both parents need to be part of the children's lives</u>

Visitation helps maintain the bond between the children and the non-custodial parent after a divorce. While it's not the same as having an intact family, in most instances a continuing relationship with both parents is important to the children's well being.

Because no one wants to feel like a visitor in his or her children's live, it can help to consider the time spent together as a parenting schedule as opposed to a visitation schedule. A reasonable parenting schedule will give your children a sense of predictability by knowing that they can maintain contact with both parents on a continuing basis.

Some of the basic areas to be covered in a visitation schedule are:

- Where will the children live during the week?
- Where will they spend weekends?
- How will holidays and vacations be handled?
- How will missed visitation be made up?
- Where and when will the children be dropped off and picked up?

<u>Typical visitation schedules</u>

A typical visitation schedule for the non-custodial parent includes every other weekend, a mid-week visit, alternating holidays, and some extended visitation during summer vacation.

The downfall with this standard schedule is that it doesn't take into consideration the age and maturity of individual children. In a divorce where both parents are willing to work together for the children's sake, a flexible parenting schedule can be worked out that shifts with the individual needs and circumstances of both parents and children.

Fixed visitation schedules

In situations where there is continuing conflict and a lack of communication between the parents, it may be a good idea to agree on a fixed visitation schedule. A fixed visitation schedule may also apply if your case has gone to trial. Below are examples of a standard visitation schedule that a judge might order.

When parents live close together:

- Every other weekend from Friday night to Sunday night (usually between 5:00 and 7:00 p.m.).

- One night per week
- Summer vacation - from two weeks up to four weeks upon notice to the primary caretaker.
- Holidays - parents will alternate holidays such as Christmas Eve, Christmas Day, New Years Day, Easter, Memorial Day, July 4th, Labor Day, and Thanksgiving. The children are usually with the mother on Mother's Day and the father on Father's Day. The children will spend the day with the individual parent on that parent's birthday.
- Child's Birthday - alternating years with each parent.

When parents live far apart:

When the parents are separated by a long distance, a court will utilize a different visitation schedule similar to the following:
- Summer vacation - six weeks each summer, with the dates to be determined by the parents.
- Christmas Break - shall be spent with the non-custodial parent from December 26th to January 3rd.
- Spring Break - alternating years between parents
- Thanksgiving - alternating years between parents
- If the non-custodial parent is visiting the children's hometown, he or she should be able to see the children as long as the custodial parent is reasonably notified. The visits shouldn't extend over 48 hours unless otherwise arranged.

Visitation needs change over time

When outlining a visitation or parenting schedule, you should take into account not only your unique situation, but also the needs of the children. With young children, a fairly rigid visitation schedule helps provide them with a consistent routine. As children get older, more flexibility will be needed as they begin to spend more time with different activities and friends.

It is unrealistic to assume that what is a reasonable schedule for a 10 year old will work well for an infant. With this in mind, you should consider including provisions for updating your parenting schedule, as the children get older. It helps to consider the different stages of a child's life when working out visitation. Remember that these are just general suggestions that can be modified to your individual situation.

Considerations for infants to six months old

It is important for young infants to have regular contact with both parents in order to continue building a close bond. To achieve this, a non-custodial parent should try to spend time with the infant three or four times a week for one to two hours. On weekends, the contact may be longer, but shouldn't last for more than four hours. If the child is being breast-fed, it is important to schedule visitation around the nursing schedule. If the child is being bottle fed, the primary caretaker should provide bottles for the visitation. All other necessities should also be provided, such as diapers, wipes, clothing, blankets, and pacifiers. You will need to be flexible in order to work around nap times.

Considerations for infants six months to eighteen months old

Contact with the non-custodial parent can extend to two or three hours during the week if the infant is not showing signs of stress, such as fretting and crying during the last half of the visit. If there is a close bond between the non-custodial parent and the child, an over-night stay may be considered if the separation from the primary caretaker is not longer than 12 hours. Overnight stays usually aren't appropriate if the child is solely breast-feeding. As above, all supplies should be sent with the child during the visit.

Considerations for toddlers to three years old

Children under three years old need a sense of predictability, so set midweek visits will be looked forward to and help maintain the parent/child bond. Children this age are better able to understand the concept of time, and can spend overnight with the non-custodial parent as long as there is not a lot of stress or separation anxiety. Having plenty of familiar toys can make the time spent more enjoyable.

Considerations for children three to five years old

At this age, children are more capable of separating from the primary caretaker for longer periods. Weekend visits can usually extend to 24 hours, with continuing mid-week visits. If mid-week visits can't be scheduled, the non-custodial parent can keep in contact with phone calls.

Considerations for grade school age children

At this age, children are usually able to adapt to a standard visitation schedule. They can spend every other weekend with the non-custodial parent with a midweek visit. With parents who are flexible and sensitive to the needs of their children, alternative visitation schedules can be worked out to fit the needs of everyone involved.

Considerations for teenagers

As children get older, they may resent the rigidity of a fixed visitation schedule. While children should not be put in the position of deciding what the visitation schedule should be, their input should be taken into consideration. If your teenager is comfortable with the set visitation schedule, that's great. If not, you may need to be more creative in finding ways to keep the teenager in contact with the non-custodial parent. Some ideas include eating out, school events, email and phone calls.

Shared Parenting

In some situations, parents are able to work out a schedule in which the children spend a relatively equal amount of time with each parent. This type of shared parenting requires flexibility and cooperation on the part of both parents. This is a really only feasible if both parent live close to each other and the children's school.

Some alternative methods of shared parenting include:

Pre-school - Alternating weekends and half the week spent with each parent provides the children with frequent contact with both mother and father.
School Age - A split week parenting schedule that includes alternating weekends and alternate weeks with each parent may work if the children can adapt to the frequent change of residence without resentment.

Don't make contact with the other parent uncomfortable

Time that is shared between the children and the non-custodial parent should occur outside of the custodial parent's home to prevent discomfort and ongoing conflict.

Visitation should be spent focusing on the children and not checking up on the other parent. Don't pump your children for information about your ex or try to interfere with the relationship they have with their father.

Along the same lines, it is important to remember that mail between the children and their father is confidential. It should not be opened, read, or kept from the children. Phone contact should not be discouraged unless it is at inappropriate times, such as when the children are sleeping.

Approach visitation like an adult

The primary custodian should provide clothing that is appropriate to the weather and activities when the children are spending time with the other parent. The custodial parent should also send along various supplies for the children such as bottles, diapers, wipes, books, toys, etc. The non-custodial parent should send the children's belongings back home with them after the visit is over.

If parents elect not to have a fixed visitation schedule, the non-custodial parent should choose reasonable hours in which to see the children. Adequate notice should be given to the custodial parent beforehand to avoid conflicting plans. If visitation plans change, it is courteous to inform the other parent and let the children know that visitation won't occur as planned. To avoid disappointment, arrangements can be made to reschedule the visitation.

Parenting Plans

When children are involved in a divorce, a well-constructed parenting plan can save many headaches down the road. Because even married parents disagree about how to raise their children, it is realistic to foresee differences of opinions concerning the children's lives after you're divorced. It is a good idea to think about the future and address any problems that might come up now. This can save a lot of conflict and help avoid going back to court at a later date.

Outlining your parenting plan

A parenting plan can outline how the different aspects of your children's lives will be handled, as well as the details of the custody, visitation, and support arrangements. You should address the following considerations when constructing a parenting plan that will fit your unique situation:

Custody - The best custody arrangements are reached mutually between the parents, but some cases require mediation or a court decision. You should outline:

•   Who will have legal custody?

_____

•   Who will have physical custody?

_____

•   If joint physical custody is decided upon, what are the timesharing arrangements?

_____

Child Support - Child support outlines the parent's obligations to support their children. Support is not a static issue, and it can change over time. Child support is usually addressed in the child support order but it can also be included as part of your parenting plan. Some things to think about are:

•   What is the level of support as dictated by state guidelines?

_____

•   Will support be higher or lower than this and why?

_____

- Will a certain amount of child support be attributed to each child, or will it be a lump sum?

_____

- How long will child support last (when the child is 18, graduates from high school, 21, or graduates from college)?

_____

- How long will support continue for a special needs child?

_____

- Will child support continue if a child attends college?

_____

- How will child support be paid (wage withholding, direct payment to the child support division, or personal payment)?

_____

- Will the parent who is ordered to pay child support register with the Child Support Enforcement Agency of your state?

_____

- What are the provisions for adjusting child support?

_____

- Will the non-custodial parent include provisions for continuing support in the event of his or her death?

_____

Visitation Schedules - A visitation schedule will need to be worked out that allows the non-custodial parent ample time with the children. Look over the section on visitation for more specific information about visitation. Here are some questions that should be addressed:

- How often will the children stay with the non-custodial parent?

_____

- Are midweek visits welcomed?

_____

- How often and when?

_____

- What are reasonable times for the non-custodial parent to call the children?

_____

- How will a change in visitation plans be handled?

_____

- Where will the children spend spring break?

_____

- How will summer vacation be handled? How much notice will the non-custodial parent give the primary caretaker if fixed summer vacation is not set?

_____

- If one parent will travel with the children, will the other parent's permission be sought?

_____

Where will the children spend the following holidays?

Christmas _____	Thanksgiving _____
Easter _____	Mother's Day _____
Memorial Day _____	Father's Day _____
July 4th _____	Child's Birthday _____
Halloween _____	Mother's Birthday _____
Labor Day _____	Father's Birthday _____

Contact With the Other Parent - It helps to outline how each parent will stay in contact with the children when they are with the other parent. It doesn't have to be a rigid schedule, but you should discuss how contact could be made. There should be an assurance that the other parent won't interfere with the contact. Below are various forms of communication. You can address how each should be handled.

Phone calls: _____

Mail: _____

Faxes: _____

Email: _____

Instant Messaging: _____

Transferring the Children - When parents are able to remain civil, dropping off and picking up the children is usually not an issue. If there is continuing conflict between the parents, it can be a good idea to specify how this will occur. You should think about:

• Is there a neutral place (such as McDonald's) that the children can be exchanged at?
_____

• Who will drop off and pick up the children, the parents or another party?
_____

• If public transportation is used, who will pay for it?
_____

• If the children have to fly, who pays for it? What will happen if the children are too young to fly?
_____

• What will be the times to drop off and pick up the children?
_____

• How will the other parent be notified if there is a change in plans?
_____

Medical Decisions - For the children's safety, both parents should be allowed to make emergency medical decisions and be required to notify the other parent in such an event. You should also try to reach an agreement on the following subjects:

• Who will be the children's health care provider?
_____

• Who will be the children's dental care provider?
_____

• Who will be the children's eye care provider?
_____

- Who will be responsible for taking the children to the doctor or dentist?

- Which parent will be required to carry health and dental insurance on the children? (Some parents agree that if insurance is offered through work, then that parent will carry the insurance.)

- Who will pay the deductible and co-payment?

- How will uncovered expenses be handled?

- Will both parents have a copy of the children's insurance policy and card?

- How will elective procedures be decided upon? Will it take the approval of both parents?

Child Care - Adequate childcare can ease the worries for both parents. It can save a lot of conflict if parents can agree on how the children will be cared for while the parents are working or away from the home.

- If the children are young, will they attend daycare or be taken care of by a babysitter?

- How will the childcare provider be chosen?

- If the children are of school age, what will be the after-school arrangements while the custodial parent works?

- If the custodial parent needs someone to watch the children occasionally, will the non-custodial parent be given the option to be called first? (This should not be used as an opportunity to judge or check up on the other parent).

Religion - There can be continuing conflict between parents if they are of different religious backgrounds. It helps to address this issue before conflicts arise.

- Under what religion(s) will the children be raised?

- If the children will be raised with both religious views, how will this be handled?

- What religious institute or church will the children attend?

- How will holidays such as Christmas, Easter, and Halloween be handled?

- If one parent's religion prohibits certain medical procedures, how will this be handled?

Education - Even though you and your spouse may agree on the general education of the children, it is wise to consider the following:

- Will the children attend public or private school? What school will the children attend?

- How will school tuition, fees and activities be paid for?

  _____

- Will both parents be involved in school conferences and parent/teacher meetings?

  _____

- Will both parents have access to school records and report cards?

  _____

- Which parent will be the designated contact person in case of emergencies at school?

  _____

- How will disciplinary problems at school be handled?

  _____

- If the child needs tutoring or special assistance, how will this be handled?

  _____

- How will the non-custodial parent be notified of school events?

  _____

- How will college be paid for?

  _____

Extracurricular Activities - Children normally have a wide range of outside activities beyond school and home. Preparing how to handle these activities can ease conflict down the road:

- Will children attend and participate in various camps and activities?

  _____

- Who will pay for these events?

  _____

- Will children participate in sporting events?

  _____

- How will team fees and uniforms be paid for?

  _____

- Will both parents abide by practice and game schedules?

  _____

- How will the non-custodial parent be notified of the various practices, games, camps, and events that the children will participate in?

  _____

Provisions for Moving - In today's world, it is common to for parents to relocate to another town for better job opportunities or to be closer to family. This can present a problem when school-age children are involved, and you should consider how it would be handled:

- Will a move by the custodial parent require a review of the custody and visitation schedule?

  _____

- What is a reasonable relocation distance that would not require a review of the custody and visitation arrangements?

  _____

- How will a move by the non-custodial parent be handled?

  _____

- Will there be prompt notification of all changes of address and phone numbers?

  _____

- How will long-distance travel by the children be handled and paid for?

  _____

- In cases of long-distance moves, how will the visitation schedule change?

  _____

Other Considerations - You may want to include other stipulations in your parenting plan that are unique to your situation, such as:

- Restrictions on the use of illegal drugs or alcohol abuse in the presence of the children.

- Not involving the children in inappropriate situations.

- Shielding the children from disagreements between you and the other parent.

- How conflicts will be handled if mutual agreement can't be reached. This may include mediation or a court hearing.

- Provisions for registering with the state child support division.

- Provisions on how delinquent child support payments will be handled.

- How will the children be claimed for tax purposes? Will parents alternate years in which they claim the deduction? Will one parent claim one child, while the other parent claims the other? Will the deduction be dependent on child support payments?

- Provisions for the continuing care and support of the children in the event of a parent's death. This can included carrying life insurance that names the children as the main beneficiaries with the other parent as the trustee.

- Provisions for an annual review of the parenting plan to make any adjustments that are necessary.

VIII
Financial Support

Child Support

<u>Children have a legal right to be supported</u>

Your children have a legal right to be supported whether you are married or not. The purpose of child support is to maintain your children's standard of living until each child reaches the age of majority. It is important to note that both you and your spouse are obligated to support your children.

Child support is generally mandatory until a child turns eighteen or graduates from high school (whichever occurs last), but may continue for longer. The amount of child support that will be ordered in your case will be determined by the child support guidelines of your individual state, taking into consideration the parent's income and the number of children to be supported.

<u>Methods for calculating child support</u>

Individual state guidelines vary, but are based on the four models described below. You can also look up your individual state in the child support table that follows this section.

- **<u>Income Shares Model</u>**
  The basis of the income shares model is that children are entitled to the same level of support that they would have received had their parents not divorced. It assumes that both parents have shared in the support of their children prior to the divorce. The incomes of both parents are combined to determine the child support obligation. Any extra childcare and medical expenses are added to this figure to reach a total child support obligation. This obligation is then prorated between the mother and the father according to their respective shares of the total income.

- **<u>Flat Percentage of Income Model</u>**
  This model determines support as a percentage of the non-custodial parent's income without taking into consideration the custodial parent's income. Under this method, the percentage of income that

will be paid toward support remains the same at all income levels, and is determined by the number of children. In some states, there is a cap on the child support obligation at the highest income levels.

- **Varying Percentage of Income Model**
  Determination of the child support is based on a percentage of the non-custodial parent's income, but will vary according to the level of income. As income increases, the percentage applied toward child support decreases (based on the fact that the cost of raising children does not increase proportionately with an increase in income). The percentage is also affected by the number of children to be supported.

- **Melson Formula Model**
  Under the Melson Formula, the standard of living of the parents is taken into consideration, allocating a certain amount of income exempt from child support (for self-sufficiency). Any income above this level for each parent is added together to determine each parent's share of support. Childcare expenses can be added to the level of support, and a Standard of Living Adjustment is added in. This helps to insure that the children's standard of living will increase along with their parent's standard of living. This is a complicated model, but in comparison to the others, it is consistent and predictable.

Under the various models, the custodial parent does not actually make support payments, but is assumed to be spending the determined level of support on the children's needs.

Parents also have the option of deviating from the guidelines as long as both parties are in agreement and the support obligation will maintain the children's standard of living. Remember that a judge will review the support agreement and may not sign an agreement that is not within a reasonable range of the support guidelines.

Adjustments to support

Child support guidelines provide a base level of support, but individual circumstances can cause the support to be higher or lower. These factors include:
- Child care expenses
- Uninsured medical and dental expenses
- Extra educational expenses such as private school tuition or tutoring
- Joint custody arrangements with split timesharing

Guaranteeing Child Support

If your ex-husband should die before the children leave home, it can put a tremendous financial burden on you. You can include a provision in your child support agreement that requires a life insurance policy be taken out or an annuity be established that will pay the child support should your ex die.

When child support ends

In most states, support obligations end when a child reaches the age of majority (age 18 or graduating from high school, whichever is reached last). If there is more than one child, whether support is decreased when the oldest child turns 18 or graduates will depend on how the support order is worded. If there was a set amount of support to be paid for each child, then the total support will be decreased at this time.

If the support orders called for a lump payment (without a set amount designated for each child), then the support will not decrease unless the issue is brought before a judge.

Other instances in which child support can end are:
- The court declares your child emancipated
- Your child gets married
- Your child joins the military
- Your child dies
- Your child moves out of the house to live independently

Modifying child support

Because custody arrangements and earning levels can change over time, child support may need to be modified at a later date. Any modifications to child support will require a judge's approval, with the change in circumstances being noted.

Child support levels can be adjusted due to certain circumstances, such as a substantial increase or decrease in income of either parent. Economic hardships, such as a disability or an uninsured catastrophic loss may be a basis for modifying child support as well. Support levels will also change if there is a change in the custody arrangements.

It is important to take into consideration any financial changes in both parents' situations when considering an adjustment. For example, a significant rise in the custodial parent's income may actually lead to a decrease in the level of support paid if the guideline percentages are followed. Always consult a lawyer's advice before taking your case back to court. It could make matters worse.

Bankruptcy may be a basis for modification of the child support, but it cannot be used to discharge any back child support obligations. It may seem strange, but the bankruptcy of the obligated parent can result in an increase in the level of support ordered due because the parent will then have fewer outstanding debts to pay.

Methods of payment

Federal law now requires that all new or modified child support orders include a wage withholding provision. This method automatically deducts the support payment from the non-custodial parent's paycheck.

Unfortunately, this doesn't work if the non-custodial parent is self-employed or doesn't hold a steady job. In these instances, child support payments can be made to an officer of the court or the child support enforcement agency in your state (which in turn sends a payment to the custodial parent).

It is a good idea to register with the child support enforcement agency of your state at the time of your divorce. This can help speed up things if there is ever a delinquency. The least advisable method of paying child support is through direct payments to the custodial parent. It is very hard to prove that payments were made or received unless you keep meticulous records. This method of payment can easily be abused.

Tracy Achen

Child Support Factors by State

Each individual state has its own guidelines to calculate support. Your lawyer should have the appropriate guidelines to determine the amount of child support that should be paid. As you can see in the chart below, there are variations on what is taken into consideration in determining support. Under the medical and child care factors, states may consider these costs as part of, or in addition to the base child support.

State	Income Shares Model	Fixed Percent Model	Variable Percent Model	Melson Formula	Medical Factor	Child Care Factor	College Support
AL	x				permissive	mandatory	x
AK		x			mandatory	x	x
AZ	x				mandatory	permissive	
AR			x		deviation factor	deviation factor	
CA	x				mandatory	mandatory	
CO	x				mandatory	mandatory	
CT	x				deviation factor		
DE				x	mandatory	mandatory	
DC			x		deviation factor	x	until age 21
FL	x				permissive	mandatory	
GA		x			permissive	mandatory	
HI				x	mandatory	x	x
ID	x				mandatory	permissive	
IL		x					x
IN	x				permissive	mandatory	x
IA	x						x
KS	x					mandatory	
KY	x				mandatory	permissive	
LA	x				mandatory	mandatory	
ME	x				mandatory	mandatory	

140

State	Income Shares Model	Fixed Percent Model	Variable Percent Model	Melson Formula	Medical Factor	Child Care Factor	College Support
MD	x				mandatory	mandatory	
MA			x		mandatory	x	x
MI	x				mandatory	mandatory	x
MN			x			mandatory	
MS		x			deviation factor	deviation factor	
MO	x				mandatory	mandatory	x
MT				x	mandatory	mandatory	
NE	x				deviation factor	mandatory	
NV		x			mandatory	deviation factor	
NH	x				deviation factor		x
NJ	x				mandatory	mandatory	x
NM	x				permissive	mandatory	
NY	x				mandatory	mandatory	x
NC	x				permissive	mandatory	
ND			x			deviation factor	
OH	x				mandatory	mandatory	
OK	x				deviation factor	mandatory	
OR	x				permissive	mandatory	x
PA	x				deviation factor	mandatory	
TX			x		mandatory	deviation factor	
RI	x				deviation factor	mandatory	
SC	x				deviation factor	mandatory	x
SD	x				deviation factor	deviation factor	
TN		x			mandatory		x
UT	x				mandatory	x	
VT	x				mandatory	mandatory	
VA	x				x	x	
WA	x				mandatory	mandatory	
WV	x				mandatory	mandatory	
WI		x			mandatory	deviation factor	
WY	x				deviation factor	deviation factor	

Child Support Enforcement

In an ideal world, no one would have to worry about missed child support payments. In the real world, delinquent child support is an all too common occurrence. It is your children's right to be supported by both parents.

It is your responsibility to protect your children's financial interests

If you don't take action when support becomes delinquent, then most likely no one else will. It is ultimately your responsibility to protect your children's financial interests and to make sure that payments are kept up to date.

The Child Support Enforcement Division

There are various methods for collecting past due child support. The first place that many people start is with their state's Child Support Enforcement Division (CSED). Federal law requires that the services of the CSED of each state be made available to anyone who requests them.

There is a nominal fee of $25 to register and there may be additional fees for court filings. If your ex registered with the CSED at the time of the divorce, it will help speed up the collection of back child support. Below is a discussion of the various methods that the state child support enforcement agencies can use to collect child support.

Wage assignments

Wage assignments are the most common method of collecting current and delinquent child support. A wage assignment order requires the obligated parent's employer to deduct the support payment from the employee's wages, and must be served on the employer before it becomes effective.

The payments are then sent to the other parent or the CSED (which in turn pays the custodial parent). Under federal law, an employer must withhold the support that is ordered. If the employer doesn't comply, such a violation can lead to the employer then becoming responsible for the payment.

Under the Consumer Protection Act, the maximum withholding from wages that can be taken for child support is 50% if the parent is supporting another child or spouse. If the parent is not supporting another child or spouse, then the withholding limit is 60%. These maximums can be increased by 5% if the support is more than 12 weeks past due.

The amount withheld may also be lowered due to a hardship such as a disability, living in poverty, or if there is a significant illness (but it won't be reduced below the monthly support obligations). If your ex is self-employed or switches jobs often, then wage withholding is not really an effective method of collecting back support and other means will need to be used.

License suspension

States have the ability to suspend or revoke personal and recreational licenses in an attempt to collect back child support. Many obligated parents who are self-employed are professionals that need a license to do business, so the threat of losing their professional license can be a powerful motivator to pay child support obligations.

Examples of licenses that can be suspended are: driver's licenses, professional and occupational licenses, hunting licenses, and fishing licenses. Usually the obligated parent is given notice of the proposed action to allow payment of the past due amount before the license is revoked or suspended.

Credit reporting

By federal law, child support agencies must report delinquent child support that is more than $1000 past due, but can also report delinquencies that are less than this amount. Having a bad mark from the CSED can prevent the delinquent parent from creating more debt that would hinder his or her ability to pay.

Seizing tax refunds

If an obligated parent's child support payments are up to date, state and federal tax refunds can't be touched to collect support. If the child support does become delinquent, then the CSED can take steps to seize federal and state tax refunds to help pay the back child support owed.

States can request an offset of a federal tax refund if the past due amount is more than $500 (or $150 if the state has provided financial assistance to the parent who is owed support). The seized refunds are turned over to the other parent unless he or she has been on public assistance.

If the parent has been on public assistance, the funds will be first applied to the state debt. Unfortunately, many delinquent parents can work around having their refunds seized by claiming fewer deductions on their tax withholding.

Attaching benefits and dividends

The CSED can have child support obligations deducted from state and federal benefits, unemployment payments, and workman's compensation. Permanent fund dividends can also be used to pay back child support, as well as garnishing military retirement benefits.

Placing liens and seizing property

The CSED also has the ability to garnish bank accounts, stock dividends, and lottery winnings. They can place liens on vehicles and income producing property, but generally won't place a lien on the delinquent parent's primary residence.

Liens are a means of preventing the owner from selling the property until the back support is paid off. Some states permit property to be seized and sold to pay off the debt, but usually won't attach property that is used to make a living.

If your ex owns a company, it can be placed in receivership with an appointed trustee to insure that the child support is paid. If the obligated parent is self-employed and living in another state (while owing at least $5000 in back support), then the IRS may seize property, attach assets, and possibly close the business.

Denial of passports

If a delinquent parent is documented as owing more than $5000 in back support, he or she may be unable to get a US passport. A passport will not be issued until the US Department of Health and Human Services (HHS) has been notified by the CSED that acceptable payment arrangements have been made. HHS will then notify the Passport Services that payment has been made and a passport can be granted (it usually takes 2-3 weeks).

Filing contempt of court charges

If you are the parent who is owed support, you can request a hearing for contempt of court. If the nonpaying parent is found guilty of contempt, the judge can order additional support payments to make up the past due amount. The judge may also require that a bond be posted or can even send the delinquent parent to jail. Interest may also be assessed on the back support.

Deadbeat parent list

Obligated parents owning more than $5000 in back child support may be listed on the Deadbeat Parent's List maintained by the Department of Social Services. This list contains names, photos, and information about the delinquent parent. There is also the Deadbeat Parent's Punishment Act of 1998 that makes the intentional failure to pay support for a child in another state a felony if the arrearage is more than $10,000, or has been unpaid for more than two years.

Offsetting public assistance

If you apply for welfare because you are not receiving child support, many states will ask that you assign your support rights to them while you are receiving assistance. The state will then try to collect the back child support to help offset the money paid in public assistance.

When you go off welfare, the money that the state collects for back support is first applied to the ongoing support obligation, next toward any delinquent support, and lastly toward anything owed to the state.

<u>Other methods of collecting child support</u>

The state attorney's office can help enforce court-ordered child support by bringing suit against the obligated parent. Private attorneys may also be used to help collect past due amounts by bringing contempt of court charges and serving wage assignment orders.

There are also private agencies that offer collection services. If you do decide to use a private child support collection agency, read all the paperwork very carefully before signing the collection contract.

While these companies can often get results much faster than the CSED, the collection fee, usually 20-30% of the support will reduce the amount of support you receive. Many collection companies will collect their percentage regardless if they or the state CSED are the ones who initiated payment.

Alimony

Alimony, also called spousal support or maintenance, is money paid by one spouse to the other after a separation or divorce to equalize the standard of living between the parties.

The purpose of alimony

Traditionally, alimony was meant to provide for the spouse who had stayed home to care for the family and did not have marketable job skills. Alimony awards today are not as common as they once were because both spouses usually work to support the family.

In most cases, alimony is awarded to enable a dependent spouse the opportunity to become financially independent. Spousal support may also be awarded to the custodial parent of preschool children, spouses in need of job training, or to older homemakers who would be unable to become self-supporting.

Alimony today also tends to be awarded more generally on a temporary basis as compared to the permanent alimony of previous eras, and may be awarded to men as well as women. Generally, alimony awards will not provide for the standard of living in which a spouse was accustomed to before the divorce.

Factors in determining alimony

For alimony to be awarded, a spouse will need to make a claim for it in the separation or divorce agreement. The following factors are taken into consideration when evaluating the basis for alimony:

- **Length of marriage** - Marriages that last longer than 10 years result in alimony awards more often than those that have lasted for only two or three years.

- **Need** - Some spouses are at a financial disadvantage because they have not ever worked outside of the home or have worked only sporadically during the marriage. It may take awhile before this spouse can gain financial independence. Some considerations for determining need are whether additional training will be needed to gain employment, whether there are very young children at home that need a parent's care, and how much money it will take for the dependent spouse to live on.

- **Manner of living** - The courts will look at the standard of living that a spouse has become accustomed to during the marriage. If you want alimony, documentation of your standard of living can help in getting a fair support agreement. This can include pictures of the house and vehicles, documentation of vacations, and a budget showing the family's normal expenditures.

- **Age and health of the spouses** - Older people generally pay more alimony than younger people due to the fact that they are more established and have more financial resources. A disabled spouse will tend to be considered more readily for alimony than a spouse who is healthy and capable of working.

- **Sacrifices made during the marriage** - If one spouse has supported the family while the other spouse received schooling or training to establish a professional career, then that spouse may be compensated for his or her contributions.

- **Ability to pay** - The courts try to balance the needs of the dependent spouse against the ability of the other spouse to pay support and still live on what's left over. Generally, a spouse living at the poverty level will not be ordered to pay alimony.

- **Premarital agreements** - An existing premarital agreement may affect the amount and type of alimony awarded. A premarital agreement that gives no alimony or only a token sum may be overruled in some states if the dependent spouse will be left with no means of support.

- **Marital fault** - Some states take into consideration marital fault when determining the alimony award. If marital fault is an issue in your divorce, look up your specific state in the following chart, and discuss the implications with your lawyer.

There are different types of alimony awards reflecting the level of support in individual circumstances. These different types of spousal support are discussed below:

Temporary alimony (alimony pendente lite)

Temporary alimony is usually ordered while the parties are separated and before the divorce is finalized. It is intended to help the financially dependent spouse continue to afford housing and pay bills until everything is settled. Sometimes a spouse will voluntarily provide financial support to the other spouse during the separation. At other times, the lawyer for the dependent spouse may request an order for temporary alimony.

Reimbursement alimony

This type of alimony is most commonly awarded in marriages where one spouse helped put the other through school and build up a professional career. Because divorce will prevent the sacrificing spouse from realizing the future benefits of this professional career, reimbursement alimony is a means of compensation for the time and effort invested during the lean years. Reimbursement alimony is not tied to needs, so it may continue indefinitely or terminate after a set amount of time (or by remarriage of the reimbursed spouse).

Rehabilitative alimony

Rehabilitative alimony is paid for a set amount of time to allow a dependent spouse the opportunity to receive training in order to earn a livable income. It may also be awarded to a custodial parent with young children not yet in school.

Rehabilitative alimony may be subject to review at the end of the alimony term (if there is a provision for review in the divorce settlement). If there is a review clause, the court will determine whether alimony should continue after the set date or upon employment.

Generally, rehabilitative alimony ends when the dependent spouse becomes employed, but is not affected by whether that spouse marries or lives with a significant other.

Permanent alimony

Permanent alimony can be awarded to a spouse who doesn't have the capability of being self-supporting. This may be the case in long-term marriages where one spouse has been a homemaker and does not have marketable job skills. It may also be awarded in cases where one spouse is permanently disabled and is unable to be self-supporting.

As the name implies, permanent alimony does not have a set time limit. There are circumstances in which permanent alimony will cease, such as when either spouse dies or the dependent spouse remarries or lives with a significant other on a permanent basis.

The following sections contain individual state factors for alimony consideration, tax implications of alimony payments, and a discussion of alimony payments, modification, and termination factors.

Alimony Factors by State

State	Statutory list of factors	Marital Fault Relevant	Standard of Living Considered	Status of Custodial Parent Considered	Lump Sum Payment Allowed
AL		x	x		
AK	x		x	x	x
AZ	x		x	x	
AR					
CA	x		x		
CO	x		x	x	
CT	x	x	x	x	
DE	x		x	x	
DC		x	x		
FL	x	x	x		x
GA	x	x	x		
HI	x		x	x	
ID	x	x			
IL	x		x	x	
IN	x				
IA	x		x	x	
KS					x
KY					
LA	x	x	x		x
ME	x				x
MD	x	x	x		
MA	x	x	x		
MI		x	x		x
MN	x		x	x	
MS		x			
MO	x	x	x	x	

State	Statutory list of factors	Marital Fault Relevant	Standard of Living Considered	Status of Custodial Parent Considered	Lump Sum Payment Allowed
MT	x		x	x	
NE	x		x	x	
NV		x	x	x	x
NH	x	x	x	x	
NJ	x	x	x	x	
NM	x		x		x
NY	x	x	x	x	
NC	x	x	x		x
ND		x	x		
OH	x		x		x
OK			x	x	
OR	x		x	x	x
PA	x	x	x		
RI	x	x	x	x	
SC	x	x	x	x	x
SD		x	x		
TN	x	x	x	x	
TX	x	x	x	x	
UT	x	x	x	x	
VT	x		x	x	
VA	x	x	x		x
WA	x		x		
WV	x	x		x	x
WI	x		x	x	
WY		x			x

Alimony Payments and Modification

Courts try to balance the needs of the dependent spouse against the other spouse's ability to pay support when awarding alimony. When both spouses work, alimony awards tend to be smaller and for a shorter length of time. Very few states have set guidelines to determine spousal support levels, but the following formula can be useful to get a rough estimate for reasonable support.

Estimating alimony payments

Computation	Here is an example:
Net income	2500.00 net monthly income
- Child support	-500.00 child support
= Adjusted net income	2000.00 adjusted net income
X 20%	X 20%
= Alimony payment	400.00 alimony payment

Establishing payments

Unfortunately, alimony payments are all too often dropped after the divorce is finalized. If you are awarded alimony in your divorce decree, there are a few things that you can do to protect yourself.

If you will be receiving alimony payments as well as child support, check with your state's Department of Human Resources or Child Support Services to establish whether both payments can be made through official channels. This will provide a clear record of payments made and received, removes direct contact between ex's, and provides the tools for collection if payments become late. You can also set up a wage assignment in which payments are made to the state collection agency.

Lump sum payments

Because many people who are ordered to pay alimony don't make payments once the divorce is finalized, you might consider a lump sum payment as compared to monthly payments. It can make sense to consider a lump sum payment because it ends the monthly reminder of a marriage gone bad and guarantees the full amount of alimony is paid.

If you choose to go with the lump sum payment, realize that the amount may be discounted because all the alimony is being paid up front. You'll need to consult with your attorney to find out if this is a viable option, because not all states allow lump sum payments.

Also, consult with your financial planner to determine the tax consequences. If the lump sum payment is classified as alimony in the divorce settlement, it will be subject to income taxes for the recipient in the year it is received. If the lump sum payment is classified as a settlement, it may not be taxable.

Alimony in gross

If your husband agrees to continue mortgage payments on the family home that you retain in the divorce, this may be considered "alimony in gross," which is actually a form of property settlement. You shouldn't have to claim the mortgage payments as taxable income, and your spouse won't be able to deduct them for tax purposes. To qualify as alimony in gross, the payments must be part of the property settlement, with payments not lasting longer than 10 years, and not be subject to termination.

Enforcement

If alimony payments become past due, you can go back to court to enforce the alimony order. Your ex-husband can face contempt of court charges and the court may also garnish his wages and seize assets to collect the alimony due.

If wages are garnished, the Consumer Credit Protection Act limits the garnishment to 50% of the earnings if he is supporting another spouse or child and 60% if not. An additional 5% can be garnished if support payments are more than 12 weeks past due.

Insuring payment

In order to protect future interests, it's worth seeking a guarantee that alimony will continue in the event of your husband's death. This can be accomplished by carrying life insurance on your husband, naming you as the beneficiary of the policy. The policy amount should be high enough to make up for any lost alimony payments due to death and should be maintained for the duration of the alimony term.

It is wise to include a provision requiring that the insurance company notify you of nonpayment of the premiums. You also have the option of paying for a life insurance policy on your husband to guarantee continuing support in the event of death.

You can also secure your future interests by requesting that a bond be posted or a trust established to guarantee that alimony payments are made. A clause can also be added to your divorce decree for a limited irrevocable assignment of income against a pension. This guarantees that alimony payments will continue by being drawn from the pension plan should regular payments become delinquent.

This provision should be included in the Qualified Domestic Relations Order (QDRO) of your divorce decree. An Alimony Substitution Trust can also be established at a bank or brokerage firm. The investments in this trust produce dividends and interest, which in effect "pay" the monthly alimony amount. If you choose to go this route, consult with a certified financial planner about the tax consequences.

Tax implications of alimony

It is important to consider that alimony payments are deductible on federal income taxes for the paying spouse, whereas child support is not. Likewise, the recipient must claim alimony as income when filing taxes. Alimony payments are taxable in the year they are received, and you can't claim alimony deductions during a tax year in which you and your spouse file a joint income tax return.

Because no taxes are withheld on alimony payments, you may need to increase the withholding from your paycheck to cover the extra taxes due at the end of the year. In some instances, alimony recipients may need to file taxes quarterly due to the alimony payments. Talk with your tax advisor for more information.

For alimony to be deductible for tax purposes, the following requirements must be met:

1. Payments must be set forth under a divorce decree or separation agreement.

2. The alimony agreement must require that payments cease upon death of either spouse.

3. The parties to the alimony agreement may not live together.

4. The parties to the alimony agreement must file their taxes separately.

5. Alimony is paid by cash or a check, not in the form of a property settlement.

Modifications

Alimony awards can be modified at a later date due to a change in circumstances. To modify alimony, the issue must be brought before the court. If the original divorce settlement prohibits modification at a later date, there may be nothing that can be done to change the level of obligation.

If the divorce settlement doesn't contain a provision for review, it may or may not be open to review. Consult with your lawyer about the review laws of your individual state. Below are some instances in which alimony can be modified:

• Remarriage or long-term cohabitation of the alimony recipient, depending on how the divorce settlement is worded.

• A decrease in the earning ability of the paying spouse due to unemployment (for more than six months), disability, or retirement.

- An increase in the recipient's financial status due to a significant wage increase, inheritance, or lottery winnings.

- Bankruptcy of the obligated spouse may subject the alimony to modification, but won't discharge past due alimony.

- Usually lump-sum alimony is a fixed payment that is not subject to modification or termination. It is usually in lieu of a property settlement and may be used as a type of reimbursement alimony.

- The death of either party will usually terminate alimony unless there are provisions in the divorce decree otherwise

IX
Wrapping Things Up

Changing Your Name

<u>Taking back your maiden name</u>

Whether or not you restore your maiden name after your divorce is a matter of personal choice. Some women choose to keep their married name to avoid confusion for their children. Others take back their maiden name to signify a clean break from the marriage. It's entirely up to you whether you change your name or not.

<u>Divorce decree provisions for assuming maiden name</u>

If you want to take back your maiden name after divorce, it is easy to have a provision added to your divorce decree to accomplish this. While you can legally change your name by usage alone, it generally makes life easier if you have court documents to support the name change. For example, you will need legal documentation of your name change if you wish to obtain a new passport or a birth certificate attachment.

<u>Changing your children's last name</u>

In some instances you may also want to change your children's last name at the time of the divorce. This can be a stickier situation because you are petitioning to change someone else's name other than your own.

A court petition may change a child's name when it is judged to be in the best interest of the child. To make this determination, the court will consider:

- The length of time that the father's last name has been used

- Whether the father has been consistently involved in the child's life

- The ties between the child and the father's extended family

- The child's ability to understand the significance of the name change

- The social impact of a particular name in the community (to help protect the child from a bad reputation)

Deciding to change a child's last name is not taken lightly, and the judge will consider all of these factors when determining whether to authorize the name change or not.

Notification of name change

If you choose to change your last name, you will need to notify all institutions and individuals that you deal with of the name change after your divorce is finalized. It's a good idea to have a certified copy of your name change documents on hand to show as proof of the change.

Since many businesses require a driver's license and social security card as proof of identity, it is best to have your name changed on these documents first. Once you have your new drivers license and social security card, you can then notify other businesses and agencies. Use the following list to help you get started:

- Employer
- Form W-4 withholding
- Passports
- Post Office
- IRS
- State Tax Agency
- Voter Registration
- Banks
- Investment Companies
- Trusts
- Contracts
- Credit Cards
- Credit Reporting Bureaus
- Organizations
- Subscriptions
- Phone Book Listings

- Insurance Companies
- Health Care Proxies
- Retirement Plans
- Living Wills
- Power of Attorney
- Property Titles
- Vehicle Titles
- Department of Records or Vital
- Statistics
- Utility Companies
- Public Assistance Office
- Veterans Administration
- Schools
- Dentists
- Doctors
- Alumni Associations

Tax Consequences of Divorce

As with everything else, divorce will also affect your taxes. It is a good idea to hire a tax consultant to go over your divorce settlement before you sign it. This is because you need to consider the tax consequences of the provisions it contains.

<u>Taxable vs. non-taxable support</u>

For example, child support is non-taxable, but alimony is taxable. Therefore, it will be more beneficial to get the majority of your support classified as child support.

<u>Capital gains and deductions</u>

You will also need to consider how much taxes will have to be paid on any assets that you sell after the divorce that have increased in value. Determining the rough capital gains on items that you will be receiving in the settlement will allow you to offset it with more money up front. You will also need to determine who will claim the children as a deduction.

<u>Filing status as determined by marital status</u>

How you file your taxes will be determined by your marital status on December 31st of the filing year. If your divorce is final by that date, then you are considered divorced for the entire year. If your divorce is not finalized before December 31st, you have the option of filing your taxes as "married filing jointly," "married filing separately," as "head of household" (if you have children).

The following section discusses some things to take into consideration on the different filing statuses if your divorce is not yet finalized.

<u>Married- filing jointly</u>: If taxes are being filed jointly, it may be wise to have any refund check sent to the lawyers office to prevent one spouse from taking the check, forging the other spouse's signature, and pocketing all of the money. Arrangements also need to be made for payment of any taxes.
* Pros: you can share exemptions, credits, and deductions such as child dependent exemptions, earned income credits, and spousal IRA contributions.

- Cons: You are jointly responsible for any tax liability, fraud, or penalties (regardless of who is responsible). If you have reason to believe that your spouse has committed fraud or will lie on the tax returns, it is wise to file separately.

Married- filing separately:
- Pros: You can avoid liability for tax fraud and penalties of your spouse, while still being able to take the dependent exemption if you have physical custody of the children.
- Cons: Only one spouse can itemize deductions if the decision is made to file this way. A decision should be made on who will get to deduct the mortgage interest, property taxes, etc.

Head of Household: To qualify as head of household, you must maintain a home and support a dependent child (or your parents) and also be separated from your spouse for at least six months.
- Pros: There is a bigger deduction and a more favorable tax rate under this filing status.
- Cons: You can only use this election if you are supporting a dependent. To be able to take the dependency exemption, the child(ren) must live with you for at least six months out of the year.

Once your divorce is finalized, you only have the option of filing as "single" or as "head of household" if you have dependents that you support.

Claiming the child deduction

If you have children, the IRS only allows one parent to claim a child as a deduction. If the non-custodial parent will be claiming one or more children as a deduction, the custodial parent will need to fill out IRS form 8332, which authorizes the non-custodial parent to use the deduction. The non-custodial parent will need to file this form with the rest of his/her tax forms.

It is important to note that the custodial parent can determine how long the deduction will be in effect for, either on a yearly basis or until a specific date. If you are the custodial parent, it is probably wise to fill out a new form 8332 every year in the event that your husband becomes delinquent on his child support payments. It can also be written into your divorce agreement that the deduction by the non-custodial parent is dependent on the payment of child support.

How support is taxed

If you are receiving child support, this is not considered taxable income for tax purposes. Alimony, on the other hand, is taxable to the recipient and a deductible expense for the payer. Once again, consult with a tax advisor before you sign your settlement agreement.

Divorce Agreement Checklist

Your divorce agreement is a written contract between you and your husband. It outlines how everything will be structured and handled when your marriage ends. It should address the following issues, as well as any other specifications of your divorce:

Issues Dealing With the Children:
- Determination of physical and legal custody
- Visitation rights and schedule
- Child support - amount, modification terms, termination provisions, methods of enforcement, wage assignment provisions.
- Parenting plan
- Insurance provisions for the children
- Determination of who will claim the children as a deduction for tax purposes
- Provisions for payment of the children's college education
- Provisions for review of custody, support, and visitation issues

Division of Assets
- Family home
- Business interests and professional degrees
- Pensions and retirement accounts
- Real Estate
- Vehicles
- Banking and investment accounts
- Stocks, bonds, annuities, and trusts
- Whole life insurance policies
- Household, shop, and outdoor items

Division of Debts
- Bank loans

- Mortgage loans
- Vehicle loans
- College loans
- Credit cards
- Liens, judgments, and collection accounts
- Other outstanding debts and private loans

Alimony

- Type of alimony
- Duration of payments
- Lump sum option
- Methods for insuring payment
- Modification provisions

Modifications Incident to Divorce

- Cobra plan allowing the uninsured spouse to continue coverage
- QDRO's on pension plans
- Tax roll-over on the sale of the family home
- Restoration of maiden name
- Life insurance to guarantee support payments
- Other securities to guarantee payment

Other

- Notification of pending bankruptcy
- Release from future debts of either spouse
- Payment of attorney fees and court costs
- Determination of tax liability
- Transfer of property, titles, and financial accounts
- Provisions for review
- A mediation clause

Finalizing Your Divorce

Once you and your husband have worked out all the details of your divorce (through negotiations, mediation, or trial), your divorce can be finalized. Your divorce settlement can be drawn up by either lawyer and will be signed by you and your spouse.

The judge needs to sign the final decree

The final judgment will include all the provisions of your divorce and will be presented to the judge for approval. Once the judge signs the final decree, your divorce will be finalized. The county clerk will then enter your divorce decree into the counties official court records.

Handling the details of your decree

You should set up a meeting, preferably at the time that you both sign the divorce settlement, to handle all the items outlined in the divorce. This will include transferring of real estate (and any quit claim deeds that need to be signed) and personal property, signing over the titles to vehicles, reversing wills, modifying insurance policies, and returning any papers belonging to the rightful owner.

Below is a list of items to be handled at the time of the divorce:
- Banks - take your name off joint accounts that you husband keeps and vise versa

- Credit cards - cancel any joint accounts

- Real Estate Papers - quit claim deeds, bill of sales, title survey, appraisals, leases, homeowners insurance policies, mortgage papers

- Vehicles - transfer titles to the rightful owner as outlined in the divorce

- Securities - assignment of stock certificates and bonds according to the divorce agreement

- Insurance - life insurance guaranteeing support payments, health insurance for the children, COBRA elections for continuing health insurance

- Promissory notes between spouses guaranteeing payments of debts

- Wage Withholding paperwork for child support or alimony

<u>Legal representation ends when the case is closed</u>

Ask your lawyer when your divorce will be finalized, and when you will receive a copy of the final decree. The representation by your lawyer ends when all the necessary paperwork is exchanged, documents recorded, and the case is closed.

Future representation for enforcement of support orders or non-compliance with the divorce decree will generally be considered a new legal matter. Therefore, new financial arrangements will need to be made at that time.

Modification and Enforcement of Your Decree

<u>Reasons for modification</u>

Your divorce decree can be modified at a later date due to a change in circumstances. The most common areas subject to change are child custody, visitation, child support (due to job loss, inheritance, death of the child, or a custody modification), and alimony (which may be modified due to job loss, remarriage, or cohabitation). Modifications will require a petition before the court and a decision by a judge to become effective.

<u>Non-compliance with the divorce decree</u>

If you were awarded property or cash payments in your divorce settlement and you husband refuses to comply, you can take him back to court on an "order to show cause". The judge will hold him in contempt of court and can possibly threaten jail time unless he complies.

If you have to take your ex-husband back to court to enforce the divorce agreement, then he may be ordered to pay for court cost and attorney's fees. This is up to the judge's discretion, and may be decided on the party's ability to pay. Other methods of enforcement include having his wages garnished, placing a lien on his property, or having his bank account seized.

<u>Enforcing child support orders</u>

If you need help collecting child support payments, you can request the services of your state's Child Support Enforcement Agency. If you have applied for public assistance, then the state automatically steps in to collect the child support to help offset the assistance the government gives. There is usually a $25 application fee, as well as additional fees for paternity tests, filing fees, parent locator services. These fees can usually be deducted from the support that is collected.

Information needed to enforce support payments

When you contact the CSE for help in collecting child support you will need the following information:

1. Children's birth certificates

2. Your child support order

3. Your divorce decree or separation agreement

4. Records of any child support previously received

5. Information on the non-custodial parent, such as:

    •   Name, address, and Social Security Number

    •   Name and address of current or recent employer

    •   Names of friends and relatives

    •   Information about his income and assets

    •   Physical description of your husband

After the Divorce

You will need to review and change a lot of paperwork once your divorce is finalized. You will find some general suggestions below to help you get started.

Changing financial records

You need to contact all institutions that you and your husband had financial dealings with to notify them of the divorce and any changes that need to be made. You should take your name off any bank accounts that your husband retained in the divorce.

Likewise, have his name taken off your accounts. This includes checking, savings, CD's, safety deposit boxes, etc. Contact the credit bureaus to update their files about your new status. For credit accounts, request that the debt be reported solely as that of the responsible party.

You should request a name change (if applicable) and an update of information for all investment accounts, mutual funds, trusts, stocks, bonds, etc. If there is a beneficiary designation, then you may want to also change this.

Insurance issues

It's a good idea to review your auto, health, and homeowner's insurance policies after your divorce to make sure that they reflect the change in your status. Also check to see that the correct person is designated as the beneficiary on your life insurance policy. If your spouse is designated as the beneficiary, you may want to change this.

Wills

Now that the property has been divided, you will need to update your will. Check your state laws to see if you will need to leave something to your ex in your will (to prevent the will from being contested in the event of your death).

You should name a trustee to insure that your assets aren't squandered and will be used to provide for the children. If your ex has relinquished parental rights, you should appoint a guardian for the children. This will insure that the person you choose raises your children.

Proxies

You should look toward whom you want to handle your affairs if you should become incapacitated. A health care proxy, living will, and power of attorney will outline who should make decisions for you if you are unable to. If you have these papers from when you were married, you may want to update them. You probably want someone other than your ex making decisions for you should you become incapacitated due to illness or injury.

Property transfers

You will need to update information on any property that you received in the divorce. For real estate, make sure that your husband signs a quitclaim deed for the property that you receive. This removes any claim to the property that he may make at a later date. Be sure to file the deed with your county court house and retain a copy for your records.

You will also need to change the insurance policies for any property that you receive. If you received any vehicles in your divorce settlement, you will need to have your ex sign over the title. Take it to the motor vehicle department to register the title in your name only.

Notifying your employer

Your employer will need to be notified if you are changing your name after the divorce so that employee records can be updated. You will also need to update your W-4 form if you will be receiving alimony.

Because alimony is considered taxable income, you may want to decrease the number of deductions claimed to offset the additional taxes you will owe.

You will also need to remove your husband's name from your pension plan unless it was addressed differently in the divorce decree.

Notifying businesses, schools, and organizations

If you have children in school, you will need to update their records, especially if you will be moving to a new address. Also make sure that the phone number is correct should the school need to contact you.

If you will be staying in the marital home, you should get all the utilities transferred into your name. Also have your name removed from any services that your husband will be keeping. This also applies to rental agreements. You will be held responsible should your ex fail to pay.

Social security benefits of ex-spouses

There are certain instances in which you may qualify for social security benefits based on your ex. To qualify, the following circumstances must apply:

- The marriage lasted at least 10 years
- You have not remarried
- You do not qualify for social security benefits based on your own earnings (you were a homemaker)
- You have been divorced for at least two years
- You must be at least 62 years old

Social security survivor benefits

Children under the age of 18 are entitled to survivor benefits if a qualifying parent dies. If your marriage lasted at least 10 years and you have not remarried, then you will qualify for widow's benefits (whether your ex has remarried or not).

Conclusion

It is my hope that this book has given you some insights into the divorce process, which will help you make good decisions before, during, and after your divorce. While going through a divorce is never easy, with the proper knowledge and the right attitude, you can make wise choices when your marriage ends. You will have many opportunities to go to war with your spouse, but it doesn't need to be this way. You can choose to civilly split your lives, do what is best for the children, and still receive a fair settlement.

While your divorce may be one of the more traumatic events that you will endure, it can also be a springboard to a fulfilling new chapter in your life. Your situation will get easier as time goes on and the bitterness fades. It will make you a stronger woman and allow you to transform your life for the better. Your future after divorce is all about identifying what you want out of life. It's also about letting go of the mistakes in your past and moving forward. Discover who you are today, what you want out of life, what's important to you, and what makes you happy. I wish you the best of luck as you journey through this new chapter of your life.

Recommended Resources - Books

A Woman's Legal Guide to Separation and Divorce in All 50 States, by Norma Harwood, J.D. Charles Scribner's Sons, 1985.

Ask A Lawyer: Divorce and Child Custody, by Steven D. Strauss. W.W. Norton & Company, 1998.

Child Custody Made Simple; Understanding the Laws of Child Custody and Child Support, by Webster Watnick. Single Parent Press, 2000.

Divorce Rules for Men, by Martin M Shenkman, J.D. and Michael J Hamilton. John Wiley & Sons, 2001.

How to Avoid the Divorce from Hell, by M. Sue Talia. Nexus Publishing Co., 1997.

How to File Your Own Divorce, by Edward A Haman. Sourcebooks, 1998.

Laws of the United States: Divorce, by Daniel Sitarz. Nova Publishing Co., 1999.

Money Smart Divorce: What Women Need to Know About Money and Divorce, by Esther Berger, CFP. Simon and Schuster, 1996.

The American Bar Association Guide to Family Law, by Jeff Atkinson. Random House, 1996.

The Best is Yet to Come, by Ivana Trump. Pocket Books, 1995.

The Divorce Decisions Workbook: a Planning and Action Guide, by Margorie L Engle and Diana D Gould. McGraw-Hill, Inc., 1992.

The Divorce Handbook: Your Basic Guide to Divorce, by James T Friedman. Random House, 1984.

The Divorce Process: Empowerment Through Knowledge, by Marlene M Browne, Esq. 1stBooks, 2001.

The Divorce Sourcebook, by Dawn Bradley Berry, J.D. Lowell House, 1996.

The Smart Divorce: A Practical Guide to the 200 Things You Must Know, by Susan T Goldstein and Valerie H Colb, Golden Books, 1999.

The Unofficial Guide to Divorce, by Sharon Naylor. Macmillian, 1998.

The Visitation Handbook: Your Complete Guide to Parenting Apart, by Brette McWhorter, Sember Sphinx Publishing, 2002.

Winning the Divorce War: How to Protect Your Best Interests, by Ronald Sharp. Allworth Press, 1998.

What Every Woman Should Know About Divorce and Custody, by Gayle Rosenwald Smith, J.D. and Sally Abrahms. Perigee Books, 1998.

Your Pocket Divorce Guide, by Linda C Senn. Pen Central Press, 1999.

Recommended Resources - Internet

ABA Network: http://www.abanet.org/family/home.html
Legal information and general public resources covering all aspects of divorce.

ADR Resources: http://adrr.com/
Articles on the various aspects of mediation.

American Academy of Matrimonial Lawyers:
http://www.aaml.org
An extensive resource of articles and resources on divorce.

Better Divorce:
http://www.betterdivorce.com/index.html
Provides information on state divorce laws, in addition to tutorials, message forums, resources, and divorce professionals.

Bolgen & Bolgen: http://www.bolgenlaw.com
Divorce Law firm in Massachusetts that has good articles on child custody support and divorce mediation.

Divorce and Money: http://divorce-and-money.com
Divorce financial planning articles.

Divorce Doc: http://divorcedoc.com/
Child custody and divorce information, laws, and resources.

Divorce Headquarters: http://divorcehq.com
Extensive articles and resources, along with a directory of divorce professionals.

Divorce Help For Women: http://www.womansdivorce.com
Articles, advice, and newsletters to help women survive the divorce process and rebuild their lives.

Divorce Helpline: http://www.divorcehelp.com
Offers a short divorce course and divorce services to help fill out your divorce paperwork.

Divorce Info.com: http://divorceinfo.com
A good site providing state divorce laws, worksheets, articles, and resources.

Divorce Magazine: http://www.divorcemag.com
This site offers state and province specific divorce information for the United States and Canada, along with extensive articles and support.

Divorce Net: http://www.divorcenet.com/
Offers legal forms, a state-by-state resource center, bulletin boards, and related family law resources.

Divorce Online: http://www.divorceonline.com
Provides free articles and information on all aspects of divorce, as well as a professional referral section.

Divorce Source: http://www.divorcesource.com
This is a huge site with discussions on specific divorce laws, articles, message centers, and resources.

Divorce Support: http://www.divorcesupport.com/index.html
Associated with DivorceSource.com, this site has a comprehensive listing of information on all aspects of divorce.

Divorce Wizards: http://divorcewizards.com
Provides divorce guidance, document preparation, mediation services, and an extensive divorce bookstore.

Free Advice:
http://family-law.freeadvice.com/divorce_law/
An excellent site offering answers to frequently asked questions about divorce.

Gary E Robbins, P.C.: http://garyrobbins.com/how_to_prepare_for_divorce_and_c.htm
This site has a good article on how to prepare for divorce and child custody.

Federal Citizen Info Center: http://www.pueblo.gsa.gov
Type in divorce into the search box for an extensive listing of divorce topics.

Mediation Matters: http://mediation-matters.com/divorce.html
This site offers a good discussion on divorce mediation.

Military Divorce Online: http://militarydivorceonline.com
A very good resource covering military divorce, offering articles, laws, and resources.

Millennium Divorce: http://www.millenniumdivorce.com
An extensive site providing articles, calculators, divorce forms, state laws, and an attorney directory.

Nolo.com: http://nolo.com/index.cfm
Click on the "Divorce & Child Custody" link on the left hand side for encyclopedia articles, FAQS, and Resources.

Smart Divorce: http://smartdivorce.com
This site provides divorce articles, reports, message boards, resources, and a personal information planner.

Support Guidelines.com: http://www.supportguidelines.com/main.html
A comprehensive resource for interpretation and application of child support guidelines in the United States.

The Coalition for Collaborative Divorce: http://nocourtdivorce.com
Offers articles on divorce and collaborative divorce, plus helpful tools and a listing of collaborative divorce professionals.

The Collaborative Divorce Lawyers Association: http://collaborative-divorce.com
This site offers a good discussion of collaborative divorce, as well as listing collaborative divorce lawyers in Connecticut.

About The Author

Tracy Achen is the author of **"DIVORCE 101: A Woman's Guide to Divorce".** She is also the creator and founder of WomansDivorce.com, a website dedicated to helping women survive divorce and rebuild their lives afterwards. Drawing from her own divorce experience and that of hundreds of other women, Tracy offers practical advice and information about the divorce process. She is a graduate of Colorado State University, and has written numerous articles on divorce and starting over. Tracy and her two sons currently reside in New Mexico.

CPSIA information can be obtained
at www.ICGtesting.com
Printed in the USA
BVHW011821160822
644724BV00012B/424

9 781418 425654